Learning English

A Guide to Grammar

von
Friedrich Ungerer, Peter Pasch,
Peter Lampater und
Rosemary Hellyer-Jones

Ernst Klett Schulbuchverlag
Stuttgart Düsseldorf Berlin Leipzig

Learning English

A Guide to Grammar

von
Dr. Friedrich Ungerer, München; Dr. Peter Pasch, Tübingen;
Peter Lampater und Rosemary Hellyer-Jones M.A., Ehingen (Donau)

Bearbeitung dieser englischsprachigen Version von
Rosemary Hellyer-Jones

Dieses Werk ist auch in deutschsprachiger Version erhältlich:
Learning English
Grundgrammatik
Ausgabe für Gymnasien
Klettnummer 51151

Gedruckt auf Papier aus chlorfrei gebleichtem Zellstoff, säurefrei.

1. Auflage 1 7 6 5 4 | 1999 98 97 96

Alle Drucke dieser Auflage können im Unterricht nebeneinander benutzt werden, sie sind untereinander unverändert. Die letzte Zahl bezeichnet das Jahr dieses Druckes.

Redaktion: Inge Schäfer, Verlagsredakteurin

Zeichnungen: Andreas Florian, Lübeck
Umschlaggestaltung: Hans Lämmle, Stuttgart
Satz: Fotosatz Kaufmann, Stuttgart
Druck: KLETT DRUCK H. S. GmbH, Korb
ISBN 3-12-511530-2

Contents

page

Chapter 7: Adverbs and adverbial phrases

Chapter 8: The tenses of the verb

Chapter 9: The passive voice – tenses and sentence patterns

Chapter 10: The auxiliaries

Chapter 16: Affirmative and negative statements, questions, shortened sentences

Chapter 17: From sentence to text (linking and emphasis)

Chapter 18: Reported speech (Indirect speech)

Appendix

Abbreviations:

N Note
AE American English
BE British English

⚠ Careful! Mistakes are commonly made here.

Chapter 1: Nouns

1 Nouns referring to persons and nouns referring to things

1. Nouns referring to persons

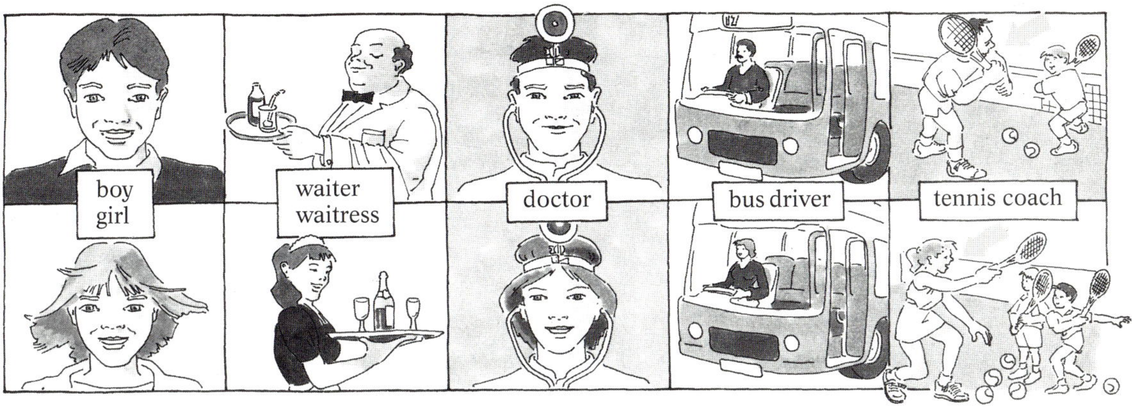

Male and female

My **grandfather** collects all kinds of newspaper cuttings, but my **grandmother** throws most of them away.
Mike used to work as a **waiter.** Now he's got his own fast food restaurant.
I once had a job as a **waitress,** too, but not for long. I kept forgetting what people had ordered.

Certain nouns refer only to men and boys, others only to women and girls.
Sometimes a suffix (usually *-ess*) is used to show that the noun refers to a female. However, this is much less common than the suffix *-in* in German.

Both sexes

Is your **friend** staying with you over the weekend? – No, I'm afraid **she** has to go back this evening.
Our **neighbour** is taking us to the station in **his** car.
Have you met my **cousin Rebecca?**
Has the **doctor** come yet? – Yes, **she**'s just arrived.

Most nouns referring to persons can be used for both sexes. This is the case with nouns such as *friend, neighbour, child, cousin, student,* etc., and most nouns referring to professions (e.g. *doctor, teacher,* etc.). It is often unclear whether the person referred to is male or female, unless a personal pronoun (*he/she*), a possessive determiner (*his/her*), or a proper name (e.g. *Rebecca*) is used. (See also § 16.2.)

Groups/Collective nouns

Are you going on holiday with your **family** this year? – No, **they**'re going in July, and I'm not free till August.

Collective nouns, such as *family, team,* etc., refer to persons seen as a group. (See also § 6.)

N 1 a **woman** doctor – a **male** nurse – a **male/female** student

The words *man/woman* or *female/male* can be used before the noun if it is important to make clear which sex is meant.

N 2 **Sammy** isn't a very good **watchdog. He** doesn't even bark at the postman.

Nouns referring to animals, especially pets, are sometimes used in the same way as nouns referring to persons. (See also § 16.2.)

2. Nouns referring to things

Singular and plural	
Where's the bread **knife**? – Here **it** is. There are no more **forks** left. **They** must be all in the dishwasher.	Most nouns referring to things can be used in the singular and in the plural, e. g. the names of objects such as *knife* and *fork*. They are called 'countable nouns'.
Singular only	
I only like **milk** to drink when **it**'s really cold. That **music** sounds lovely. Who is **it** by?	Some nouns can be used only in the singular, e. g. the names of substances such as *milk*, and a large number of abstract nouns (e. g. *music*). They are called 'uncountable nouns'.
Plural only	
These **stairs** are rather dangerous, aren't **they?** Please put your **clothes** away in the cupboard. Don't leave **them** all on that chair.	Other nouns can be used only in the plural and have no singular form, e. g. certain nouns referring to things that consist of several parts, such as *stairs* and *clothes*.

N Peter Miller – the Thames – the Alps – England – London – Oxford Street – Buckingham Palace

Proper names can refer to either persons or things (e. g. rivers, mountains, countries, etc.).

§ 2 The singular and plural forms of nouns

1. Plural with *-s*

Singular	Plural with *-s*	
one shop	two shops	[-s]
one park	two parks	
one tree	five trees	[-z]
one garden	two gardens	
one church	four churches	[-ɪz]
one bridge	three bridges	
one potato	lots of potatoes	
one tomato	some tomatoes	
But:		
one photo	several photos	

The plural of most English nouns is formed by adding an *-s*.
Pronunciation is as follows:

- [-s] after a voiceless consonant [p, t, k, etc.]
- [-z] after a vowel or a voiced consonant [b, d, g, m, n, etc.]
- [-ɪz] after a sibilant [s, z, tʃ, dʒ, ʃ] (always spelt *-es*).

Remember the pronunciation of *house* [haʊs], *houses* [ˈhaʊzɪz].

Nouns ending in *-o*, *-f(e)*, *-y*
In most cases, *-o* becomes *-oes* in the plural.

But the *-o* in *disco, photo, piano, radio* and *video* becomes *-os* in the plural.

Singular		Plural with *-s*	
one leaf my life	[-f]	two leaves our lives	[-vz]
But:			
one roof	[-f]	all the roofs	[-fs]
one baby one boy		two babies three boys	

The plural of most nouns ending in *-f* or *-fe* is formed with *-ves*.
But the plural of *roof, proof, chief* and *handkerchief* is formed by adding an *-s*.

After a consonant, *-y* becomes *-ies* in the plural. After a vowel, however, *-y* remains unchanged in the plural.

N lorry drivers, school teachers, grown-ups, drive-ins, five-year-olds, stopovers

The plural of compound nouns is usually formed by adding an *-s* to the last word.
Exceptions: *sons-in-law, sisters-in-law* (Schwiegersöhne, Schwägerinnen), *passers-by* (Passanten).

2. Other plural forms

Singular		Plural with vowel change	
one man	[mæn]	two men	[men]
one woman	['wʊmən]	two women	['wɪmɪn]
one foot	[fʊt]	two feet	[fi:t]
one tooth	[tu:θ]	32 teeth	[ti:θ]
one goose	[gu:s]	several geese	[gi:s]
one mouse	[maʊs]	a lot of mice	[maɪs]

Singular		Plural with *-(r)en*	
one child	[tʃaɪld]	two children	['tʃɪldrən]
one ox	[ɒks]	two oxen	['ɒksən]

Singular	Plural with no change
one sheep	fifty sheep
one fish	hundreds of fish
one deer *(Reh/Hirsch)*	some deer *(Rotwild)*

N bacillus [bə'sɪləs] – bacilli [bə'sɪlaɪ]
crisis ['kraɪsɪs] – crises ['kraɪsi:z]
phenomenon [fə'nɒmɪnən] – phenomena [fə'nɒmɪnə]

Some nouns taken from Latin and Greek keep their original plural form in English.

§ 3 Nouns used only in the singular (uncountable nouns)

Nouns referring to substances, such as *milk* and *coal*

We've got some **milk**, and some **bread** and **cheese** for supper.
Where did you put the **fruit** we got at the market? – Here ***it is.***
I really must wash my **hair.** ***It looks*** terrible.
Gas *is* used for heating and cooking in a lot of British homes.
Years ago, when rooms were heated by open fires, a lot more **coal *was*** used.

English nouns referring to substances are generally used in the same way as their German equivalents. However, some have a plural form in German but not in English.
Compare: *fruit* – Obst, Früchte; *hair* – Haar, Haare; *coal* – Kohle, Kohlen.

N These sweets taste of different **fruits.** – Diese Bonbons schmecken nach verschiedenen Obstsorten.
Waiter: 'Two **coffees.** Anything else, please?' – ‚Zwei Kaffees ...'

Some nouns referring to substances have a plural form, but the meaning is not quite the same:
fruits – types of fruit, *breads* – types of bread, *cheeses* – types of cheese
two coffees, two teas – two cups of coffee/tea, *two lemonades* – two glasses of lemonade

Nouns referring to a collection or group of things, such as *luggage* and *furniture*

Let me carry the **luggage.** ***It's*** so heavy. — ... **das Gepäck** ... ***Es ist*** ...
The **furniture** in this window ***is*** nice. — **Die Möbel** ... ***sind*** ...
But look how expensive ***it is.*** — ... wie teuer ***sie sind.***

Luggage (AE *baggage)* is used in the singular, like *Gepäck* in German. *Furniture* and *machinery* are also used only in the singular, unlike the plural forms *die Möbel* and *die Maschinen* in German.

Abstract nouns such as *information* and *advice*

The **information** in this leaflet ***isn't*** very interesting. — Die **Informationen** ... ***sind*** nicht ...
But the **advice** we got at the travel agent's ***was*** quite helpful. — Aber die **Ratschläge** ... ***waren*** ...

Unlike their German equivalents, *information* and *advice* can be used only in the singular.
Further examples: *homework* – Hausaufgabe(n), *knowledge* – Wissen, Kenntnis(se), *progress* – Fortschritt(e), *evidence* – Beweis(e).
Many abstract nouns, however, are used in the same way in both English and German: e. g. *courage* – Mut, *music* – Musik, *geography* – Geographie.

Nouns ending in *-s* such as *news, mathematics, darts, the United States*

Let's switch TV on. The **news** ***is*** coming on now.
Die **Nachrichten** ***kommen.***
Maths (Mathematics) ***is*** my favourite subject. I really enjoy ***it.***
Darts ***is*** a very popular game in Britain.
The United States (The USA) ***has*** a large Spanish-speaking population.
Die USA ***haben*** ...

Although these nouns end with a plural *-s*, they refer to something that is seen as a unit (e. g. 'the USA' as a country), and they are therefore used like singular nouns.

'Have you got all your luggage?'

§ 4 Nouns used only in the plural

'Ladies' clothes are on the first floor, madam.'

Nouns referring to things made of several parts, such as *clothes* and *stairs*

Ladies' **clothes *are*** on the first floor, madam.	Damen**bekleidung *ist*** im ersten Stock.
The **stairs *are*** over there on the right.	Die **Treppe *ist*** dort drüben rechts.

Unlike their German equivalents, *clothes* [kləʊðz] and *stairs* are used only in the plural.
Further examples: *goods* – Ware, *wages* – Lohn, *surroundings* – Umgebung, *thanks* – Dank.

Nouns referring to things made of two identical halves, such as *trousers*

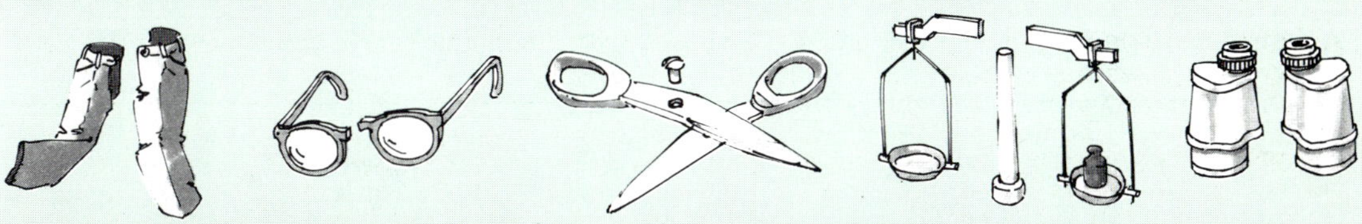

Your new **trousers *are*** nice. Where did you buy ***them?***	Deine neue **Hose *ist*** schön. ...
These **shorts *are*** too small.	Diese **kurze Hose *ist*** zu klein.
Where ***are*** my **glasses**? – ***They're*** here!	Wo ***ist*** meine **Brille**? – Sie ***ist*** hier.

Because they refer to things made of two halves, these nouns are always used in the plural, unlike their German equivalents.
Further examples:
jeans, *pyjamas* – Schlafanzug, *scissors* – Schere, *scales* – Waage, *binoculars* – Fernglas.

Nouns with plural meaning such as *people* and *police*

These days most **people *have*** a telephone.	
The **police *are*** very helpful in emergencies.	Die **Polizei *ist*** ...
They can be called day and night.	***Sie kann*** ... gerufen werden.

These nouns refer to a group, and although they have no plural ending, they are used like plural nouns, with verb forms and pronouns in the plural.

N The Spanish are ***a*** proud **people.** — ... ***ein*** stolzes **Volk.**
A prayer was said for all the **peoples** of the world. — ... alle **Völker** der Erde ...

People can also mean 'nation' or 'race' (*Volk* in German). In this case, it can be used in both the singular and the plural.

§ 5 Expressions of quantity with nouns used only in the singular or only in the plural

Nouns used only in the singular or only in the plural cannot be used with the indefinite article or with numbers, because they are uncountable (exception: *four people*).
There are different ways of expressing quantity with these nouns.

Different expressions of quantity with different substances

a **piece of** [əv] cake
a **packet of** tea
a **bottle of** milk
a **pound of** butter
a **cup/pot of** tea
a **bar of** chocolate
eine Tafel Schokolade

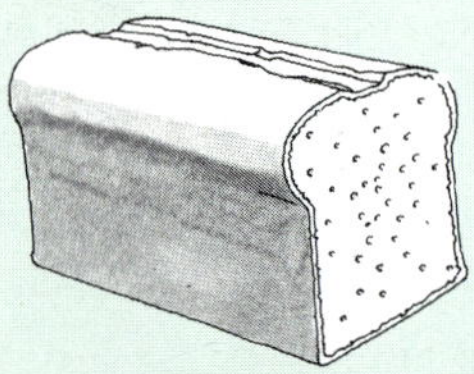

⚠ a **loaf of** bread
ein (Laib) Brot

a **slice of** bread
ein(e Scheibe) Brot

Pair(s) of **with things made of two halves**

a **pair of** glasses
eine Brille
two **pairs of** pyjamas
zwei Schlafanzüge
two **pairs of** scissors
zwei Scheren
five **pairs of** shorts
fünf Paar Shorts

Piece(s) of **with concrete and abstract singular nouns**

a beautiful **piece of** furniture
several **pieces of** luggage
a good **piece of** advice
ein guter Rat
an interesting **piece of** information
eine interessante Information

Some **and** ***any*** **as expressions of quantity**

I need **some** advice. I wonder if you could help me.	Ich brauche (einen) Rat.
I asked about local buses at the tourist office. But they couldn't give me **any** information.	Aber man konnte mir keine Auskunft geben.
Have you got **any** scissors? I'd like to cut out this advert.	Hast du eine Schere?

Some and *any* can be used with all the above nouns.
See § 23 for the use of *some* and *any.*

§ 6 Collective nouns such as *family/team*

Family and a number of other collective nouns have singular and plural forms (*one family, two families*), unlike *people* and *police* (§ 4).
When used in the singular, however, they can be used in two different ways.

My **family *are*** always together at Christmas time.

My **family *is*** one of the oldest in the town.

A group seen as a number of individuals: verb, pronoun and determiner in the plural	**A group seen as a unit: verb, pronoun and determiner in the singular**
Our school **team *are*** away in London at the moment. ***They are*** playing in the National Cup. The **crowd *were*** so angry that ***they*** started throwing bottles onto the field.	Our rugby **team *isn't*** very strong this year. ***It needs*** a new coach. There ***was*** an enormous **crowd** outside the football ground, waiting to get tickets.
Here the emphasis is on the members of the group and their activity as individuals. In English, a group such as a family, team or crowd is very often seen in this way. Other common examples of such groups are: *class, club, crew, audience, government, school, company.*	Here the emphasis is on the group as a whole. In this case, as in German, the group is seen as a unit.

N 1 A large **number of** patients **are** still waiting for treatment.
Half of the children **were** ill. (But: **Half of** the money **was** spent on new equipment for the hospital.)

A number of and *the majority of* are always followed by a plural noun, and the verb is also used in the plural. (In English, unlike in German, the verb form does not depend on the expression of quantity itself, but on the noun following it.) *Half of* can be followed either by a plural noun (+ verb in the plural), or by a singular noun (+ verb in the singular).

N 2 A hundred pounds **is** a lot of money.
Five years **is** a long time to wait.

After sums of money, periods of time and other measurements, even when they are in the plural, the verb usually appears in the singular. This is because the sum, period or measurement is seen as a unit.

N 3 **Everybody** ***sends their*** love. ***They*** all ***miss*** you.

In colloquial English, the indefinite pronouns ending in *-body* and *-one* are often used in combination with the plural forms *their* and *they*. However, the verb immediately following *everybody, someone,* etc. must be used in the singular.

§ 7 *s*-genitive and *of*-phrase

1. Form and pronunciation of the *s*-genitive

Singular		
Kate's	book	[keɪts]
Father's	pipe	[ˈfɑːðəz]
Charles's	records	[ˈtʃɑːlzɪz]
Alice's	cassettes	[ˈælɪsɪz]

Singular nouns take an apostrophe + *s*.
Pronunciation is as follows:
[-s] after a voiceless consonant [p, t, k, etc.]
[-z] after a vowel or a voiced consonant [b, l, etc.]
[-ɪz] after a sibilant [s, z, tʃ, dʒ, ʃ]

Plural		
my parents'	books	[ˈpeərənts]
the boys'	room	[bɔɪz]
the children's	toys	[ˈtʃɪldrənz]
men's	clothes	[menz]

Plural nouns ending in *-s* take an apostrophe only.
Other plural forms take an apostrophe + *s* (like singular forms).
The pronunciation follows the rules given above. (See also § 2.)

⚠ My **friend's** [frendz] bike is new.
My **friends'** [frendz] bikes are over there.
My **friends** [frendz] all live in town.

Remember (for listening comprehension):
Nouns with a regular plural ending sound the same, whether they are genitive singular, genitive plural, or ordinary plural forms. They can only be distinguished by paying attention to the context.

N Mrs **Jones's/Jones'** hats [ˈdʒəʊnzɪz/dʒəʊnz]
the **Bates's/Bates'** house [ˈbeɪtsɪz/beɪts]

Surnames ending in *-s* (e. g. *Jones, Bates*) can take the apostrophe with or without *s*.

2. The use of the genitive

s-genitive for persons and animals	*of*-phrase for things
I've brought **Ronny's guitar.** He left it behind at **the Browns' party.** Where's **Spot's basket**? Don't take **the dog's biscuits** away – it might bite!	There's a big supermarket in **the centre of the town.** The car park is at **the other end of the High Street.** Let's put the bags in **the back of the car.**
For persons, the *s*-genitive is used in nearly all cases (see the box on the right for exceptions). The *s*-genitive is also usually used for animals (even in cases where the animal would be referred to as 'it').	The *of*-phrase expresses a certain relationship between things (the way something 'belongs' to something else). The *of*-phrase is also used when the description of a person or persons is very long, e. g.: *Is that the house* ***of those people that we met at the tennis club yesterday?***

N The Titanic was **Britain's** biggest and most modern passenger ship.
The **Government's** report will be published tomorrow.
This is **yesterday's** newspaper, not **today's.**

The *s*-genitive is also often used with places, countries and institutions, as well as with times (such as *yesterday* and *today*). It is also found in expressions such as *an hour's walk* – ein einstündiger Spaziergang, *a two days' stay* (also: *a two-day stay)* – ein Aufenthalt von zwei Tagen.

§ 8 The *s*-genitive without a noun

Noun already mentioned

That's a nice **camera.** – It's **my mother's.** I've only borrowed it.

Whose **bike** is that outside? – It must be **Peter's.**

The noun that would normally follow the *s*-genitive can be left out if it has already been mentioned. This is especially the case after questions with *whose.*

Expressions such as *at the butcher's*

We get our meat **at the butcher's** in Queen Street.
Where's Tim? – He's **at David's/at the Longs'.**
I have to go to **the doctor's** tomorrow.
St Paul's isn't far from the Tower.

In the case of shops, people's homes, restaurants and well-known buildings, the noun that would normally follow the genitive (e. g. *shop, house, cathedral)* is understood without being mentioned at all. The genitive stands alone here.

'But I told you to go to the newsagent's today, not to the butcher's.'

N The new headmaster is **a friend of my father's.** ... ein Freund (unter mehreren) meines Vaters.
Compare: The new headmaster is **my father's friend.** ... der (einzige) Freund meines Vaters.

The 'double genitive' in *a friend of my father's* is a combination of the *of*-phrase and the *s*-genitive. This construction expresses the idea that the father probably has several friends. The ordinary *s*-genitive in *my father's friend* suggests that the father may have only one friend.

Chapter 2: Articles, demonstrative pronouns and determiners

§ 9 The definite article

1. Forms and pronunciation

the [ðə]	the [ðɪ]
the **p**lane the **f**light the **n**ew airport	the **I**rish plane the **e**arly flight the **a**irport
the **Eu**ropean airlines [ˌjʊərə'pi:ən] the **U**nited States [jʊ'naɪtɪd]	
	the **h**our ['aʊə] before your flight the **S**AS [ˌes eɪ 'es] plane

The form of the definite article is always *the.*
The pronunciation is [ðə] before consonants, and [ðɪ] before vowels.

Pronunciation depends on the first **sound** of the following word, **not** on the **spelling.**
The article is pronounced [ðə] before [jʊ].

It is pronounced [ðɪ] before mute *h,* and when spelling the letters *f, h, l, m, n, r, s* and *x.*

N 'Suntours' is **the** ['ði:] company for cheap flights to the Continent.

If the definite article is particularly stressed, it is always pronounced ['ði:] (with a long [i:]).

2. The use of the definite article

Houses are so expensive today. **But:** **The houses *in that area*** are very expensive.

The definite article *the* is used when referring to specific or particular things or persons.
The example on the right refers to particular houses, **not** to houses in general.
The cannot be used when referring to houses in general, as in the example on the left.

Nouns used in a general sense: without *the*	Nouns describing a particular case: with *the*
Substances and abstract ideas	**Substances and abstract ideas**
A lot of **wine** is produced in California. **Mexican food** is very popular in Texas. **History** is full of disasters. **Die** Geschichte ... **Life** isn't always easy. **Das** Leben ...	**The wine we had last night** came from California. **The food in that Mexican restaurant** was excellent. I'm very interested in **the history of the American Indians.** I'm reading a book about **the life of Columbus.**
When referring to things in general, these nouns are used **without** the definite article, even if an adjective (e. g. *Mexican*) comes before the noun.	When these nouns are more closely defined (by a defining relative clause, an expression of place, or an *of*-phrase), they are used **with** the definite article.
Institutions and means of transport	**Institutions and means of transport**
School starts again in September. **Die** Schule ... The Smiths go to **church** most Sundays. ... in **die** Kirche. John and Peter go to school by **bus.** ... mit **dem** Bus ...	**The school Tracey goes to** is in Silver Street. **The church over there** was built in the last century. I must have left my camera on **the bus.**
The definite article is **not** used when referring to the **function** of the institution (e. g. lessons, church service) or the form of transport.	The definite article is used when referring to a particular school, church, etc. (usually the building itself) or to a particular vehicle.
Months, days of the week, meals	**Months, days of the week, meals**
In Britain, **July** and **August** are the most popular months for holidays. **Der** Juli und **der** August ... The working week starts on **Monday.** ... **am** Montag. When we were on holiday, we made **breakfast** ourselves, but we usually went out for **dinner.**	**The June of 1987** was unusually cold and wet. I'll never forget **the Monday I started my first job.** **The breakfast you made this morning** was the best I've ever had. **The dinner on your birthday** cost us over £ 60.
These nouns are used **without** the definite article when they are used in a general sense (for times or meals that come again and again).	The definite article is used when referring, for example, to a particular June, a particular Monday, or a particular breakfast or dinner.

N 1 **Most** cars have seat-belts at the back these days. — **Die meisten** Autos ...
Most people think we are crazy to buy such a big car. — **Die meisten** Leute ...

Most, unlike *die meisten* in German, is used without *the* when it means 'the majority of'.

N 2 Do you play an instrument?
– Yes, I play **the** piano and **the** guitar. — Ja, ich spiele Klavier und Gitarre.

Unlike in German, the names of muscial instruments are normally used **with** the definite article after the verb *play.*

§ 10 The definite article with names

The Browns and the Robinsons are neighbours.

In English, the definite article with names (including geographical names) is much less common than it is in German. However, this is only the case with singular forms.

Without *the*	With *the*
Names of persons in the singular	**Surnames in the plural**
Julie often goes to the cinema with **Peter.** **Grandma** and **Aunt Mabel** watch a lot of TV. Poor **Dad** missed his favourite sports programme yesterday. **Der** arme **Papa** ...	**The Browns** and **the Robinsons** are neighbours. Browns und Robinsons sind Nachbarn. **The Chapmans** haven't got a TV set. They seem to prefer radio.
Names of persons in the singular (including nouns used as names for relations) do **not** take the definite article. This is the case even when an adjective comes before the name (see last example).	Surnames in the plural are always used **with** the definite article.
Names of countries in the singular, and (individual) mountains	**Names of countries in the plural, and mountain ranges**
Ben Nevis is the highest mountain in **Scotland,** and **Snowdon** is the highest in **Wales.** **Mount Whitney** in **America** is about as high as **Mont Blanc** in **France.**	Many people from **the Netherlands** live in **the United States.** Skiing has become quite popular in **the Scottish Highlands,** but of course it's better in **the Alps.**
Most names of countries in the singular, and the names of most mountains are used **without** the definite article. (Exceptions: the United Kingdom, the Sudan.)	All geographical names in the plural (e.g. the names of countries and mountain ranges) take the definite article.

Without *the*	**With *the***
Lakes	**Rivers and seas**
People say that **Ullswater** is the most beautiful of the English lakes, but **Lake Windermere** is more popular for sailing. **Loch Lomond** is the largest of the Scottish lakes.	**The Thames, the Humber** and **the Tyne** all flow into **the North Sea.** **The Dover Strait** is the narrowest part of **the English Channel.**
Buildings, streets and parks	**Names containing an *of*-phrase**
Most tourists want to see **Buckingham Palace.** **Oxford Street** is London's most popular shopping street. **Hyde Park** is London's largest park.	**The Palace of Westminster** is another name for **the Houses of Parliament.** Carisbrooke Castle is on **the Isle of Wight.** Many famous people were prisoners in **the Tower (of London).**
But: **the** High Street, **the** King's Road (in London)	Names that contain an *of*-phrase always take the definite article. Names referring to very famous sights are sometimes used without the *of*-phrase.

11 The indefinite article

1. Forms and pronunciation

a [ə]	**an** [ən]
a **f**light a **l**arge airport a **U**S plane a **E**uropean airline	an **i**nternational flight an **a**irport an **S**AS plane an **h**our's trip

The indefinite article has two forms: *a* [ə] before consonants, *an* [ən] before vowels.
The form depends on the first **sound** of the following word, **not** on the **spelling.** (See also § 9.)

2. The use of the indefinite article

Unlike in German, the indefinite article is used when referring to a person as a member of a certain group (e.g. of a profession, nationality or religion).

With *a/an*	**Without *a/an***
Professions	**Titles**
Frank's father is **a policeman.** ... ist Polizist. Sally worked as **a shop assistant** last summer. ... als Verkäuferin.	Mr O'Neil has been **mayor** for at least three years now. ... ist ... Bürgermeister. Elizabeth II became **Queen** when her father died in 1952. Not many people would like to be **President** of the USA.
Nationality, religion	
Carmen Smith is **a Spaniard,** but her husband is **an Englishman.** ... ist Spanierin, ... ist Engländer. Paul is **a Catholic,** but his girlfriend is **a Protestant.** ... ist Katholik, ... ist Protestantin.	The indefinite article is not used, however, before titles which can only be held by one person (in one particular town, country, etc.). In this case, the person is not seen as a member of a group.

N 1 Carmen is Spanish, but her husband is English.

To express nationality, an adjective can be used instead of a noun.

N 2 Ben was in **a** hurry, as he always is. ... war in Eile ...
He has got **a** headache. ... hat Kopfschmerzen.

The indefinite article is used in certain expressions (such as *in a hurry, to have (got) a headache*) where the German equivalent would be without the article.

§ 12 The indefinite article with units of quantity and time

The indefinite article in the sense of *per* (= German *pro/je*)	
With weights and measures	**With units of time**
How much are these apples? - 50p **a pound.** ... 50p pro/je/das Pfund. This French wine costs £ 15 **a bottle!** ... £ 15 pro/je/die Flasche.	We don't use the car more than two or three times **a week.** ... zwei- oder dreimal in der Woche. There's a speed limit of 70 miles **an hour** on British motorways. ... 70 Meilen pro Stunde ...

§ 13 The position of the definite and the indefinite article

As in German, the definite and the indefinite article usually come before an adjective + noun (*the old book, an old book*, etc.). However, there are some exceptions:

The definite article after *half, all, both, twice, double*	**The indefinite article after *half, what, quite, such* and *rather***
We spent **half the** afternoon practising for the concert. ... den halben Nachmittag ... Sorry, **all the** tickets are sold. ... alle Karten ... **Both the** plays sound interesting. Beide Stücke ... Last week we sold **twice the** number of tickets - and made **double the** amount of money. ... die doppelte Anzahl ... den doppelten Betrag.	Let's just sit in the sun for **half an** hour. ... eine halbe Stunde ... **What a** lovely day! Was für ein schöner Tag! This good weather is **quite a** surprise. ... eine ziemliche Überraschung. We had **such a** cold winter last year that the river froze over. ... einen so kalten Winter, ...

N This is **too** difficult **a** text for me to translate.

The indefinite article also comes after *too* + adjective.

§ 14 Demonstrative pronouns and demonstrative determiners

This book, **that** shop

This, that, these and *those* can be used before nouns. In this case, they are called demonstrative **determiners.**

This is my book. Whose is **that?**

This, that, these and *those* can also be used alone. Then they are called demonstrative **pronouns.**

1. Forms and pronunciation

Singular:	**this** boy	**that** girl
Plural:	**these** boys	**those** girls

⚠ Notice the difference in pronunciation between *this* [ðɪs] and *these* [i:z].

2. The use of demonstrative pronouns and determiners

This – that **and** ***these – those*** **to express a difference or contrast**

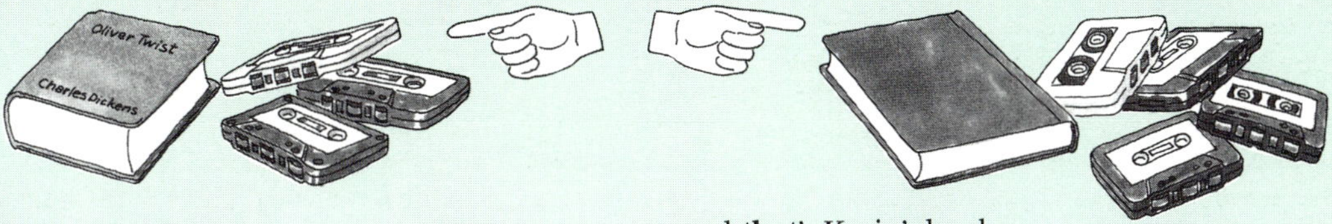

This is my book .... and **that**'s Kevin's book.
These are my cassettes........................ and **those** are Kevin's cassettes.

To distinguish between two persons or things, *this* is generally used first, and then *that* is used. In the plural, *these* is used first, then *those.*

N **This/That** is my book.

If it is not necessary to make any distinction, either *this* or *that* can be used.

This/these **to refer to what is nearer**	***That/those*** **to refer to what is further away**
Nearer in distance	**Further away in distance**
This car (here) looks pretty new	**That** car (on the other side of the street) must be at least twenty years old.
How much are **these** stop-watches here on the counter?	How much are **those** models over there?
Nearer in time	**Further away in time**
Earlier **this** year, we flew to Paris for a short holiday. Anfang dieses Jahres ... Airports are such crowded places **these** days. Flughäfen sind heutzutage ...	The last time we had been in Paris was in 1970. **That** was a long time ago. Air travel wasn't so popular in **those** days. Flugreisen waren damals ...

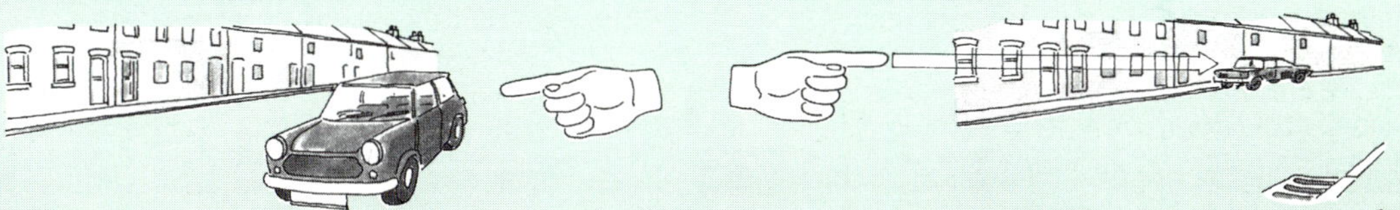

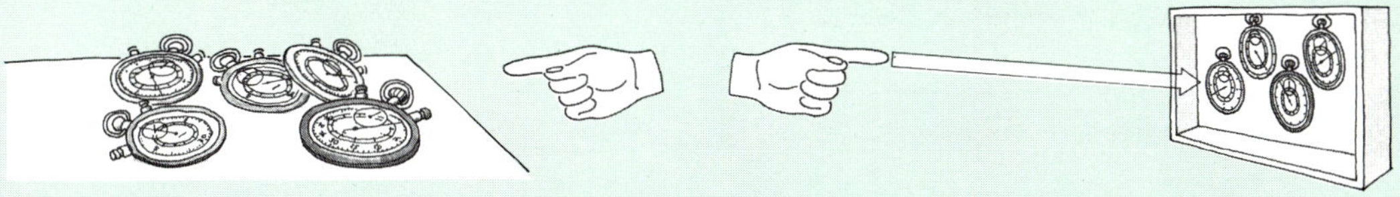

Chapter 3: Personal pronouns and determiners

§ 15 Table of forms

		Personal pronouns		Possessive determiners and pronouns		Reflexive pronouns	Reciprocal pronouns
Singular	1st person	**I**	**me**	**my** address	**mine**	**myself**	
	2nd person	**you**	**you**	**your** home	**yours**	**yourself**	
	3rd person	**he**	**him**	**his** hobbies	**his**	**himself**	
		she	**her**	**her** age	**hers**	**herself**	
		it	**it**	**its** name		**itself**	
	General pronoun	**one**	**one**	**one's** friends		**oneself**	
Plural	1st person	**we**	**us**	**our** school	**ours**	**ourselves**	
	2nd person	**you**	**you**	**your** teachers	**yours**	**yourselves**	**each other / one another**
	3rd person	**they**	**them**	**their** jobs	**theirs**	**themselves**	

§ 16 Personal pronouns

1. The use of subject and object forms

Most personal pronouns have different subject and object forms.

The subject forms (*I, he,* etc.) correspond to nominative forms in German (*ich, du, er,* etc.). The object forms (*me, him,* etc.) correspond to accusative forms in German (*mich, dich, ihn* etc.) or to dative forms (*mir, dir, ihm,* etc.).

Compare: I'll give **her** (*ihr* – dative) the book when I next see **her** (*sie* – accusative).

The object form is also used in the following cases, where the nominative form would be used in German:

'Who's that?' – 'It's only me.'

The object form after the verb *be*	
It's **me,** Barbara.	**Ich** bin's, Barbara.
That must be **him.**	Das muß **er** sein.
You needn't worry. It's only **us.**	... **Wir** sind's nur.

In colloquial English, the object form is used after the verb *be*.

The object form in comparisons

I hardly recognized Ben. He's as tall as **me** now.
... so groß wie **ich.**
Peter's good at basketball, but I'm better than **him** at swimming. ... besser als **er** ...
The Johnsons have got a bigger house than **us.**
... ein größeres Haus als **wir.**

In colloquial English, it is normal to use the object form of the pronoun after comparisons with *as* and *than*.
However, when a verb comes after the pronoun, the subject form is used: *He's as tall as **I** am.*

2. The use of *he, she, it*

He/she **for persons, *it* for things**

he: boy, husband, uncle, actor, boyfriend, etc.
she: girl, wife, aunt, actress, girlfriend, etc.
it: letter, newspaper, book, literature, etc.

he/she:
When I came in, the **shop assistant** asked me what I wanted. **He/She** was very helpful.

Unlike the German pronouns *er/sie/es, he* and *she* can only refer to persons, and *it* only to things.

Many nouns are the same for both males and females. Often the use of the pronoun makes it clear which sex is meant. (See also § 1.)

The use of *he/she/it* for animals

Just look at **Kitty. She**'s caught another mouse!
This is **Leo. He**'s the oldest lion in the zoo.

It is usual to call animals *he* or *she* if one has a special relationship to them (e.g. if they are pets). These animals usually have names.

A cat isn't much trouble. **It** looks after **itself** most of the time.
Who does **this dog** belong to? This is the second time I've seen **it** in the garden today.

In all other cases, *it* is used.

N What do you think of **my new car**? Isn't **she** (it) a beauty?
The Titanic was on **her** (its) first voyage across the Atlantic Ocean when **she** (it) hit an iceberg and sank.

She can also be used for certain things to which the speaker has a special relationship, e.g. cars and ships.

§ 17 General personal pronouns (*one, you*,etc.)

One **and *you* as equivalents of German *man***

One can't believe everything **one** reads in the paper. Man kann nicht alles glauben, ...
One shouldn't change **one's** mind too often.
Man sollte seine Meinung nicht zu oft ändern.
He may be speaking the truth, but **you** never know. ..., aber man kann nie wissen.

The pronouns *one* (*one's* in the genitive) and *you* refer to people generally, including the speaker.
In spoken English, *you* is more commonly used.
(See § 37 for the use of *one* as a prop word.)

They and _people_ as equivalents of German _man_

They say that schooldays are the happiest days of your life. What rubbish! Man sagt, daß ...
They're building a new science block next to the school hall.
People don't realize how much work goes into producing a school play.

They or *people* is used to refer to other people generally, **not** including the speaker.
(It is also common to use passive sentences as equivalents of German sentences with *man*: see § 79–81.)

§ 18 Possessive determiners

1. Forms

my jacket	**our** shoes
your scarf	**your** boots
his jeans/**her** blouse	**their** clothes
its tail	

⚠ Remember the difference between the form *its* and the short form *it's (= it is)*.
Compare:
*the city and **its** parks*
*Let's go to the park. **It's** open all day.*

2. The use of possessive determiners

Possessive determiners (also known as possessive adjectives) are generally used in the same way in English and in German. In the following cases, however, they are used in English where they would normally not be used in German.

Possessive determiners with parts of the body, clothes, etc.

The other day a friend of mine fell off **his** motorbike and broke **his** leg.	... fiel ... **vom** Motorrad und brach sich **das** Bein.
He also hit **his** head and injured **his** left arm.	... **den** Kopf ... **den** rechten Arm.
You won't need **your** coat in the car,	... **den** Mantel ...
but don't forget to fasten **your** seatbelt.	... **den** Sicherheitsgurt ...

N Over sixty people lost **their lives** in the plane crash.
... kamen ... **ums Leben.**
We've changed **our minds** about the advantages of those cheap flights.
Wir haben unsere **Meinung** ... geändert.

Possessive determiners are also used with *life* and *mind*. If the subject of the sentence is in the plural, it is necessary to use the plural forms *lives* and *minds*.

§ 19 Possessive determiners + *own*

The possessive determiners *my, your,* etc. can be given extra emphasis by adding *own*.
Unlike *eigen* in German, *own* can be used only after a possessive determiner (**never** after an article).

They haven't got a TV set of their own.

They haven't got a TV set of their own.

The two constructions with *own*
Fortunately, we've got { **our own** beach hut. / a beach hut **of our own.**
⚠ He swam out to rescue the child, but he paid for it with **his own** life. ... mit **dem eigenen** Leben.
I haven't got a surfboard **of my own.**
Ich habe **kein eigenes** Surfbrett.

The possessive determiner + *own* can be used

– before the noun
– after the noun, as part of an *of*-phrase.

Before *own*, a possessive determiner **must** be used. German expressions such as *ein eigener, der eigene, kein eigener* cannot be translated into English word for word.

⚠ an own goal   ein Eigentor

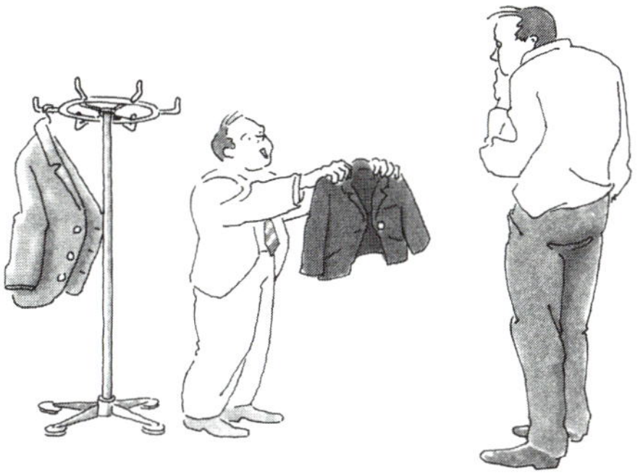

Is this yours?

20 Possessive pronouns

1. Forms

Whose book is this?
– It's ... { **mine/yours/his/hers** / **ours/yours/theirs**

2. The use of possessive pronouns

Possessive pronoun instead of possessive determiner + noun	
That's a nice **camera.** Is it **yours?**	(instead of: Is it **your camera?**)
Whose is this blue **anorak?** – It's not **mine.**	(instead of: It's not **my anorak.**)
Whose are these **cassettes?** – They're **ours,** and the **recorder** is **ours,** too.	

Possessive pronouns are used in order to avoid repeating a noun that has already been mentioned. They are especially common in answers to questions with *whose.*
(See also § 8 for the *s*-genitive used without a noun.)

N Linda is away at the moment. She's staying in London with a cousin **of hers.**
(Compare: This isn't our boat. It belongs to a friend **of my father's.)**

In this case, *of* with a possessive pronoun is used in the same way as the 'double genitive' (see § 8).

21 The pronouns ending in *-self/-selves*

1. Forms

Singular	**myself**	**yourself**	**himself** **oneself**	**herself**	**itself**
Plural	**ourselves**	**yourselves**	**themselves**		

⚠ Notice the difference between the singular form *yourself* [-f] and the plural form *yourselves* [-vz].

N The form *oneself* is used in a general sense (see § 17 for the use of *one*). It is particularly common as part of the infinitive, e.g. as given in dictionaries: *to help oneself – sich bedienen.*

2. Use

Reflexive use

While he was making the sandwiches,	
he cut **himself** with the bread knife.	... schnitt er sich ...
'May I introduce **myself?** My name's Smith.'	‚Darf ich mich vorstellen? ...'
'You can help **yourselves.** The drinks are on the table.'	‚Ihr könnt euch bedienen. ...'

The pronoun ending in-*self*/-*selves* can be used as an object. This is the case in sentences where subject and object refer to the same person or thing. The pronoun 'refers back' to the subject, and is therefore called 'reflexive'.

⚠ In German, the reflexive pronoun is sometimes the same in form as the personal pronoun. But in English, the reflexive pronoun always has a different form:

He introduced **us.** **Er** stellte **uns** vor. **We** introduced **ourselves.** **Wir** stellten **uns** vor.

Personal pronoun **Reflexive pronoun**

Reflexive in German but not in English

This is my Uncle Fred. Do you **remember** him?	... **Erinnerst** du **dich** an ihn?
Oh yes, of course. He hasn't **changed** a bit.	... Er hat **sich** überhaupt nicht **verändert.**

Reflexive pronouns are not used as commonly in English as they are in German. A large number of reflexive verbs in German correspond to verbs that are **not** reflexive in English:

sich erinnern an	remember	*sich ereignen*	happen	*sich bewegen*	move
sich (ver)ändern	change	*sich beeilen*	hurry	*sich öffnen*	open
sich fürchten	be afraid	*sich etw. vorstellen*	imagine s.th.	*sich setzen*	sit down
sich entschuldigen	apologize	*sich freuen auf*	look forward to	*sich fragen*	wonder

Emphatic use (= *selbst* in German)	
We hope that **the Queen *herself*** will come to open the new town hall.	... die Königin selbst ...
The building *itself* isn't very beautiful, but the grounds are lovely.	Das Gebäude selbst ...
The architects even designed some of the furniture ***themselves.***	Die Architekten ... selbst ...

In order to give special emphasis to a noun in a sentence, a pronoun ending in *-self/-selves* can be placed directly after it. To give stress to the subject, it is also possible to put the emphatic pronoun (*-self/-selves*) at the end of the sentence (see last example).

22 Reflexive pronouns and reciprocal pronouns *(each other/one another)*

Reflexive pronoun: ***sich selbst* in German**	**Reciprocal pronoun:** ***sich gegenseitig, einander* in German**
	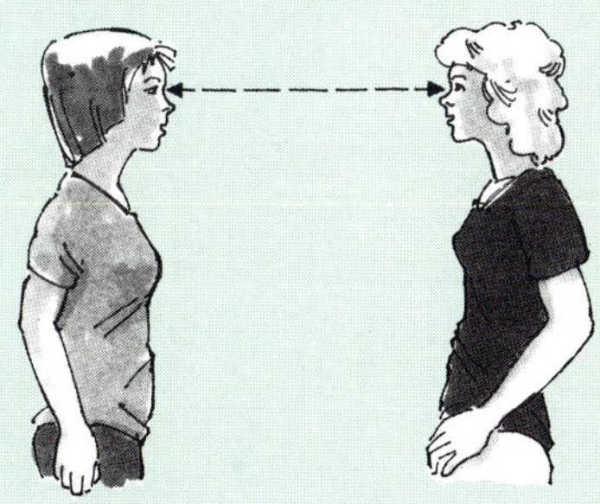
They are looking at **themselves** in the mirror. Sie schauen **sich** im Spiegel an.	They are looking at **each other.** Sie schauen **sich** an.
Animals feed their young ones until they can feed **themselves.** ... bis sie **sich** selbst ernähren können.	People would be a lot happier if they understood **one another** better. ..., wenn sie **sich** besser verstehen würden.
We ought to buy **ourselves** a really good pair of binoculars. Wir sollten **uns** ... kaufen.	We (Susan and I) haven't seen **each other** for years. Wir haben **uns** schon jahrelang nicht gesehen.
Reflexive pronouns (ending in *-self/-selves*) refer back to each individual, or to the group as a whole. There is no 'exchange' between persons or things.	Reciprocal pronouns (*each other* or *one another*) are used when there is an 'exchange' between persons or things. Reflexive pronouns cannot be used in this case.

Chapter 4: Indefinite pronouns and determiners

§ 23 *Some* and *any* used as expressions of quantity

1. Meaning

Some and *any* for German *etwas, ein paar*	
There's **some milk** on the kitchen table – and there are **some biscuits** in the cupboard. Es ist (etwas) Milch auf dem Küchentisch – und es sind (ein paar) Kekse im Schrank. Is there **any orange juice** left? Ist noch (etwas) Orangensaft übrig?	*Some* and *any* are used in English to refer to an indefinite quantity or number. ⚠ In English, unlike in German, the expression of quantity cannot normally be left out.
I've still got **some homework** to do. We don't have to learn **any words** today.	*Some* and *any* are used before nouns referring to substances, before other uncountable nouns (see §§ 1 and 3), and before nouns in the plural.
I've used up all my **writing-paper.** Have you got **any?** – Yes, of course. I'll give you **some.**	The noun can be left out if it has already been mentioned.

N 1 I need **some salt.** [s(ə)m 'sɔ:lt] – There's **some** ['sʌm] on the table.

The pronunciation of *some* is usually unstressed (the vowel sound is pronounced either [ə] or not at all). But if the noun is left out, the pronunciation is stressed (with the vowel sound [ʌ]).

N 2 **Some man** ['sʌm 'mæn] rang up this morning and wanted to speak to you. — Irgendein Mann rief ... an ...
She lives in **some village** ['sʌm 'vɪlɪdʒ] in the north of England. — ... in irgendeinem Dorf ...

Here *some* refers to a person or thing that is not known to the speaker. When used in this sense, *some* is always stressed. (See § 28 for *any* in the sense of German *jeder beliebige.*)

2. The use of *some* and *any* in different types of sentence

Affirmative statements: *some*	Negative statements: *any*
Let's buy **some** bacon for breakfast tomorrow. We've still got **some** eggs. I'd like **some** of those local-grown tomatoes, please.	I'm afraid I **didn't** get **any** peaches today. The Browns **never** eat **any** meat at all. There's **hardly any** coffee left.
	Any, not *some*, is used in negative statements. Negative meaning can be expressed by *not*, or by words such as *never, hardly, scarcely (= kaum)* and *rarely.*

Questions with *some*	Questions with *any*
Could I have **some** biscuits?. – Certainly. Here you are. Would you like **some** more tea? – Yes, please.	Have you got **any** chocolate biscuits? – Yes, I think so. Is there **any** tea left in the pot? – No, I'm afraid it's all gone.
Some is used in questions if the speaker expects or would like to hear an affirmative answer. Questions with *some* are in fact requests, offers or suggestions; they are **questions only in form**.	*Any* is used if the speaker does not know whether the answer will be *yes* or *no*. Questions with *any* are **genuine questions**.

24 The compounds of *some* and *any*

The compounds of *some* and *any* are:

someone/anyone *somebody/anybody*	(irgend) jemand
something/anything	(irgend) etwas
somewhere/anywhere	irgendwo

These compounds are used according to the same rules as *some* and *any* (see §23.2).

'Have you got anything to declare?'

Compounds with *some*	Compounds with *any*
In affirmative statements	**In negative statements**
There's **someone** at the door. Who can it be? There's a parcel for you, Mum. It must be **something** from Grandma. The Browns live **somewhere** near the post office.	There is**n't anyone** at home, I'm afraid. We **hardly** hear **anything** from Uncle Ron these days. They **never** go **anywhere** without that awful dog.
In questions intended as requests, offers, etc.	**In genuine questions**
Could **someone** pass me the butter? Would you like **something** to drink?	Did **anyone** ring up this afternoon? Is there **anything** I can do to help?

⚠ Is there **anything interesting** on at the theatre this week? ... etwas Interessantes ...?
Let's go **somewhere else.** ... woanders ...

The compounds of *some* and *any* can be followed by an adjective, or by the word *else*.

N 1 See §28 for *anyone/anybody, anything, anywhere* in the sense of *jeder beliebige, alles, überall* in German.

N 2 Other compounds of *some* and *any* are:
sometimes (manchmal); somehow (irgendwie); anyhow (irgendwie, jedenfalls, trotzdem); anyway (jedenfalls, trotzdem).

§ 25 *No* and its compounds

no* + noun – *none	
We've got **no paper** and **no envelopes.** How many **postcards** did you buy? – **None.** ... – Keine. **None of the shops** here sells stamps.	*No* for German *kein* can only be used before a noun. *None* [nʌn] is used to avoid repeating a noun that has already been mentioned. *None* is also used in *of*-phrases.
Compounds with *no*	
We rang their number, but **no one / nobody** answered the phone. Have you heard anything from Andrew? – No, **nothing** at all. I've been looking for his last letter, but it's **nowhere** to be found.	Like *some* and *any*, *no* is also used in compounds: *no one/nobody* niemand *nothing* ['nʌθɪŋ] nichts *nowhere* nirgends
The use of *not ... any* instead of *no*	
There were**n't any** telephone calls for you. (There were **no** telephone calls for you.) I **don't** remember **anything** about it. (I remember **nothing** about it.)	*No* and its compounds have the same meaning as *not ... any* and its compounds. The construction with *not ... any* is usually preferred, however. It sounds less formal.

§ 26 *Much* and *many*

Much (viel): **with uncountable singular nouns**	***Many (viele):*** **with countable nouns in the plural**
How **much money** do you spend on books? – Not **much.** I wouldn't like to study history, it's too **much work.** I didn't do **much** today.	I haven't bought **many books** so far this year. Do you read **many short stories** at school? – No, not **many.**
Much is used with nouns referring to substances, and with other uncountable singular nouns. It is also used without a noun in a general sense (= *viel* or *vieles* in German).	⚠ *Many* (= *viele* in German) is used with countable nouns in the plural. *Much* cannot be used here.

N Hurry up, we have**n't** got **much** time.
I wonder why Jo spends so **much** money on clothes.

Don't worry, we've got **plenty of** time.
We spend **a lot of / lots of** money on records.

Much is mainly used in questions and negative statements. In affirmative statements, *much* is normally only used after *so, too* and *very.* Otherwise, it is avoided, and substitute forms such as *a lot of, lots of* and *plenty of* are used instead.

27 *Little, a little – few, a few*

little (*wenig*) / *a little* (*ein wenig*) } **with singular nouns**	*few* (*wenige*) / *a few* (*einige*) } **with nouns in the plural**
I don't eat much in the mornings. I have too **little time.** There's only **a little milk** left for breakfast.	I took over thirty **photos.** – So **few?** We took at least two hundred. We bought **a few postcards** too, of course.
Little and *a little* are used with uncountable singular nouns, e.g. with nouns referring to substances.	⚠ *Few* and *a few* are used with countable nouns in the plural. *Little* and *a little* cannot be used here.

N They make very **little** money out of that hotel.
They have very **few** guests.
(They **don't** make **much** money out of that hotel, and they have**n't many** guests.)

It's only a small hotel, but they make **a little** money out of it. There are always **a few** guests.

Little and *few* (**without** the indefinite article) stress the basically negative idea that a quantity or number is very small (= *almost none at all*). In colloquial English, they are normally only used after *very, too, so* and *how.* Otherwise they are avoided, and *not much/not many* are used instead.
A little and *a few* (**with** the article) stress the more positive idea that a small quantity or number actually exists (= *better than none at all*).

§ 28 *Every, each* and *any* for German *jeder*

German *jeder* can be used in several different senses. Its equivalent in English can be either *every, each* or *any,* according to the meaning.

every: generally, or without exception

Every dog needs exercise.
Every dog owner knows that.

Jim loves animals. He knows the name of **every cow on the farm.**
Sarah goes riding **every weekend in the summer.**

Every (always followed by a noun) is used
- in general statements (*every dog = every dog in the world, without exception; each* cannot be used here).
- in statements about a limited number (*each* can also be used here: ... *each cow on the farm, ... each weekend in the summer*).

Ben is such a friendly dog. **Everyone** loves him.
He's clever too. He understands **everything** I say.
Has anyone seen Tigger? I've looked **everywhere,** but I can't find him.

The compounds of *every* are used in a similar way:

everyone/-body	jeder (alle, ohne Ausnahme)
everything	alles (ohne Ausnahme)
everywhere	überall (an allen Orten)

each: emphasis on the individual person or thing in a group

Each of the hotel rooms has a sea view.
Each of these paths goes down to the beach.

Each is especially common before *of*-phrases. (*Every* cannot be used here.)

The large **ice-creams** are 80p **each.**
He gave the **children each** a bar of chocolate.

Unlike *every, each* can refer back to a noun that has already been mentioned.

Each/Every room in the hotel has its own TV set.
We had fresh fruit **each/every day** at breakfast.

Each is sometimes used as an alternative to *every. Each* is preferred, however, when the emphasis is on the **individual** person or thing, not on the group generally.

any: unspecific example ('it doesn't matter which')

If you aren't sure of the way, ask **any person** you happen to meet.
Any time you are in our part of the town, come and see us.
You can take **any of the buses** going to Stockport. It doesn't matter which.

Any is used for German *jeder* when referring to an **unspecific** example (*it doesn't matter which*), and **not** to a particular person or thing. In this sense, it is possible to use *any* in affirmative sentences, especially in imperatives and in sentences with *can, may* and *will.* (See § 23.2, however.)

Anybody/Anyone will be able to tell us the way to the station.
I would do **anything** for you.
I don't know where the keys are. They may be **anywhere.**

The compounds of *any* can also be used in this sense:

anyone/-body	jeder	= jede beliebige Person
anything	alles	= egal was
anywhere	überall	= an jedem beliebigen Ort

29 *All*

All the neighbours love music.

all **without the article**	***all*** **with the article**
All children like sweets. Alle Kinder ... **All meat** should be kept in a cool place. Jedes Fleisch...	**All the children in our street** have got bikes. Alle Kinder in unserer Straße ... Tommy has left most of the vegetables, but he's eaten **all the meat (on his plate).** ... das ganze Fleisch ...
All without the article refers to everybody or everything within an unlimited number or amount (here: *all children everywhere/meat of all kinds*). It is especially used in general statements.	*All the* refers to everybody or everything within a limited number or amount (here: not *all children everywhere* but *only the children in our street;* not *meat of all kinds* but *only the meat on the plate*). *All* can also be used before demonstrative or possessive determiners: *all those houses* alle diese Häuser *all that money* all das Geld *all my life* mein ganzes Leben

N He worked **all day.** ... den ganzen Tag.

All without the article can be used before nouns referring to time (e.g. *day, night, afternoon, week*), to express length of time. In most other cases, however, *all* is used only with plural forms (*children, houses,* etc.) or with uncountable nouns (*meat, money,* etc.).

§ 30 *Both, either, neither*

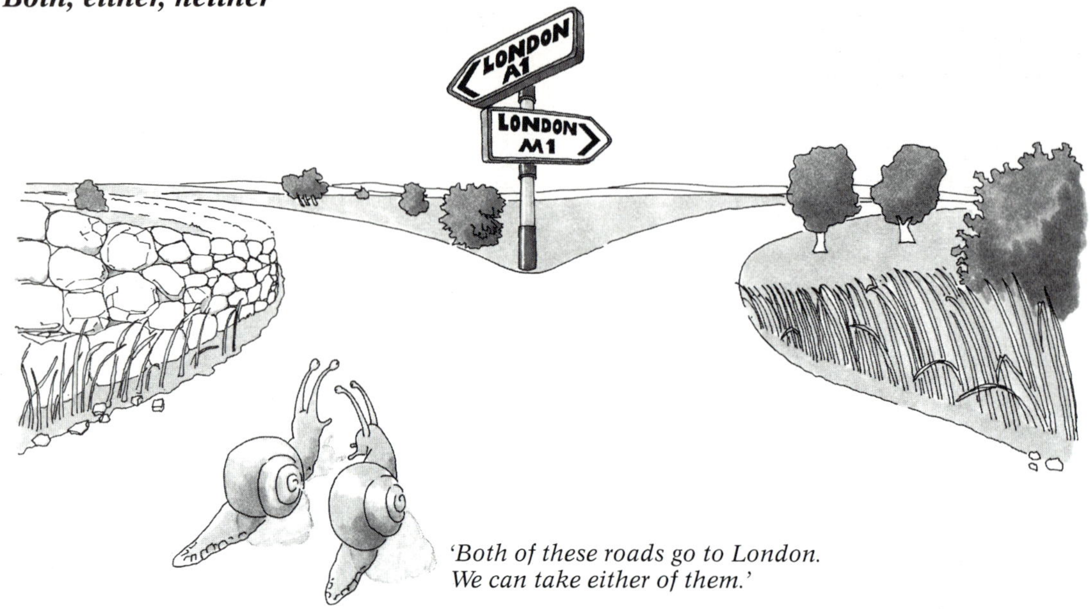

'Both of these roads go to London. We can take either of them.'

both: **one (of two) and the other**	***not ... either:*** / ***neither:*** } **not one (of two) and not the other**
Both cars were badly damaged in the accident. Beide Autos ... **Both drivers** had to be taken to hospital. Beide Fahrer ... **Both of them** were injured. Beide waren verletzt.	Which of the two cars we looked at did you like best? – I'm afraid I **didn't** like **either** of them. **Neither** of them had much room at the back. Welches der beiden Autos ...? – ... keines von beiden. Beide hatten nicht ...
⚠ The parents were both injured, but fortunately **the two children** were not hurt. ... die beiden/die zwei Kinder ...	***either:*** **one (of two), it doesn't matter which**
Unlike German *beide*, *both* is always stressed, and is **never** used after the definite article. The English equivalent of *die beiden/die zwei* is *the two*; it is not possible to use *both* here.	Shall we have green or blue seats? – I don't think it matters much. **Either** colour would look nice. Jede der beiden Farben würde .../Beide Farben würden ...

N See also §§ 144 and 145.2 for *not ... either* and *neither* as equivalents of German *auch nicht*.
See § 145.1 for *either ... or ... (entweder ... oder ...)*, *neither ... nor ... (weder ... noch ...)* and *both ... and ... (sowohl ... als auch ...)*.

Chapter 5: Numbers and expressions of time and place

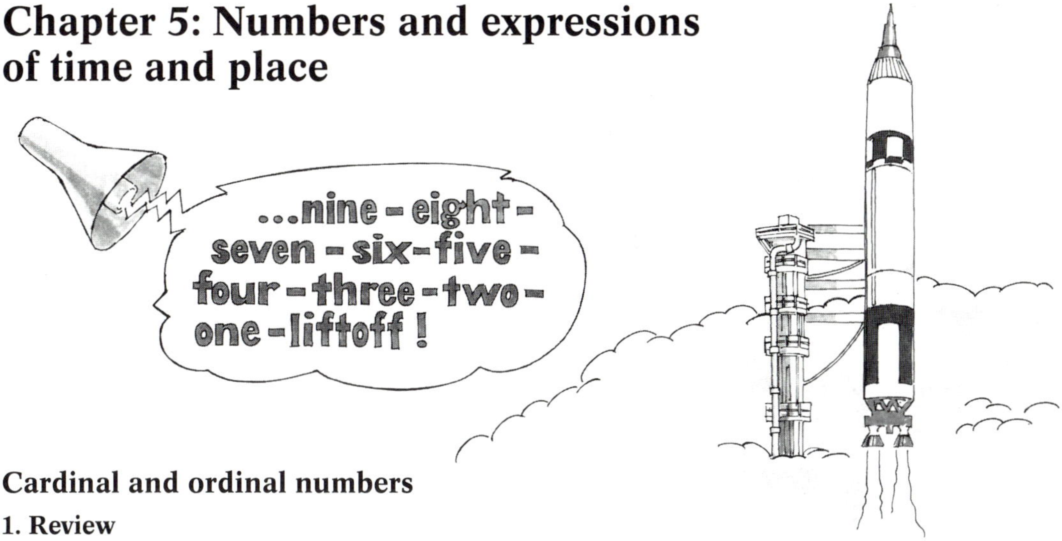

31 Cardinal and ordinal numbers

1. Review

Cardinal numbers			Ordinal numbers		
1	one	[wʌn]	1st	the first	[fɜ:st]
2	two	[tu:]	2nd	the second	['seknd]
3	three	[θri:]	3rd	the third	[θɜ:d]
4	four	[fɔ:]	4th	the fourth	[fɔ:θ]
5	five	[faɪv]	5th	the **fifth**	[fɪfθ]
6	six	[sɪks]	6th	the sixth	[sɪksθ]
7	seven	['sevn]	7th	the seventh	['sevnθ]
8	eight	[eɪt]	8th	the **eighth**	[eɪtθ]
9	nine	[naɪn]	9th	the **ninth**	[naɪnθ]
10	ten	[ten]	10th	the tenth	[tenθ]
11	eleven	[ɪ'levn]	11th	the eleventh	[ɪ'levnθ]
12	twelve	[twelv]	12th	the **twelfth**	[twelfθ]
13	thirteen	['θɜ:'ti:n]	13th	the thirteenth	['θɜ:'ti:nθ]
14	fourteen	['-'-]	14th	the fourteenth	['-'-]
15	**fifteen**	['fɪf'ti:n]	15th	the fifteenth	['-'-]
16	sixteen	['-'-]	16th	the sixteenth	['-'-]
17	seventeen	['--'-]	17th	the seventeenth	['--'-]
18	**eighteen**	['-'-]	18th	the eighteenth	['-'-]
19	nineteen	['-'-]	19th	the nineteenth	['-'-]
20	twenty	['twentɪ]	20th	the twentieth	['twentɪəθ]
21	twenty-one	[ˌ--'-]	21st	the twenty-first	[ˌ--'-]
22	twenty-two	[ˌ--'-]	22nd	the twenty-second	[ˌ--'--]
...			...		
30	thirty	['θɜ:tɪ]	30th	the thirtieth	['θɜ:tɪəθ]
40	**forty**	['fɔ:tɪ]	40th	the fortieth	['---]
50	**fifty**	['fɪftɪ]	50th	the fiftieth	['---]
60	sixty	['sɪkstɪ]	60th	the sixtieth	['---]
70	seventy	['sevntɪ]	70th	the seventieth	['----]
80	**eighty**	['eɪtɪ]	80th	the eightieth	['---]
90	ninety	['naɪntɪ]	90th	the ninetieth	['---]
100	a/one hundred	[ə'hʌndrəd]	100th	the (one) hundredth	
143	a/one hundred **and** forty-three		143th	the (one) hundred **and** forty-third	
1,000	a/one thousand	[ə'θaʊznd]	1,000th	the (one) thousandth	
4,638	four thousand six hundred and thirty-eight		4,638th	the four thousand six hundred and thirty-eight	
1,000,000	a/one million	[ə'mɪljən]	1,000,000th	the (one) millionth	
2,000,000	two million		2,000,000th	the two millionth	
1,000,000,000	a thousand million (BE) a billion (AE)		1,000,000,000th	the thousand millionth (BE) the billionth (AE)	

2. Notes on the use of cardinal numbers

thirty-two — zweiunddreißig seventy-three — dreiundsiebzig	A hyphen is used to link the words *one, two, three,* etc. to *twenty, thirty,* etc.
a hundred **and** two — hundert(und)zwei two thousand **and** twenty zweitausend(und)zwanzig	The word *and* is used to link *hundred* and *thousand* to the lower numbers (from *one* to *ninety-nine*). (In American English, however, *and* is often left out.)
a hundred pounds — (ein)hundert Pfund **one** thousand miles **two** hundred kilometres	The indefinite article *a,* or another number (e.g. *one, two*), must always be used before *hundred* and *thousand.*
50,000 (fifty thousand) — (Ger. 50 000/50.000) 4,635,826 — (Ger. 4 635 826/4.635.826) 3.5 (three point five) — (Ger. 3,5 – drei Komma fünf)	Unlike in German, numbers above 1000 usually take a comma (not a full stop) after every three digits. Decimals, however, are marked with a full stop (also called the 'decimal point').
1066 (ten sixty-six) 1994 (nineteen ninety-four)	Years are often spoken as two numbers (one for the century, e.g. *ten,* and one for the year of that century, e.g. *sixty-six*).

N According to its function, the figure 'O' can be called:

zero	['zɪərəʊ]	for the bottom of a scale: *the temperature is ten below zero.*
nought	[nɔ:t]	for the number 'O' in mathematics: *Three minus three leaves nought* (BE)/*zero* (AE).
o	[əʊ]	in telephone numbers: *55040 (double five – o – four – o).*
nil	[nɪl]	for sports results: *The match ended 5 : 0 (five nil).*
love	[lʌv]	in tennis scoring: *15 : 0 (fifteen love).*

3. Notes on the use of ordinal numbers

the first, the twenty-second, the hundred and third, the fourth, the fifth, etc. the twentieth ['twentɪəθ]	*First, second* and *third* are irregular forms. They are also used with compound numbers ending in 1, 2 and 3 (e.g. *the twenty-second*). All other ordinal numbers end in *-th.* **Note:** The spelling/pronunciation of 5th, 8th, 9th and 12th is irregular (see Review on p. 35); the *-ty* of *twenty, thirty,* etc. becomes *-tieth,* with two syllables.
1st – fir**st** 2nd – seco**nd** 3rd – thi**rd** 4th – four**th** 21st – twenty-fir**st**, etc.	When ordinal numbers are written as figures, the last two letters of the word appear after the figure (unlike in German, where a full stop is used).
Henry VIII (Henry the Eighth) Elizabeth II (Elizabeth the Second)	Roman numbers after the names of rulers (e.g. kings and queens) are written without a full stop. They are pronounced as ordinal numbers (e.g. *the Eighth*).
1/3 a/one third 2/3 two thirds 7/8 seven eighths	In fractions, ordinal numbers are used for the denominators. (Exceptions: 1/2 – *a half,* 1/4 – *a quarter,* 3/4 – *three quarters.*)

N Henry VIII wanted a divorce for more than one reason: **first(ly),** he needed a son; **second(ly),** he had become tired of his first wife and was now in love with Anne Boleyn; and **third(ly),** he wanted to break with Rome and become head of the English Church himself. **...erstens...zweitens...drittens...**

In discussions, etc. ordinal numbers are sometimes used when listing a number of points or arguments. Often *-ly* is added (e.g. *firstly*).

32 The date

How the date is written	How the date is spoken
June 2nd, 1994; June 2, 1994; 2nd June(,)1994; 2 June(,)1994; 2/6/94; 2.6.94	'June the second, nineteen ninety-four'; 'The second of June, nineteen ninety-four'

N Notice the difference in the writing of the date between British and American English.

BE: 24. 12. 94 (day, month, year)

AE: 12. 24. 94 (month, day, year)

33 Expressions of frequency

The Queen opens Parliament **once** a year.
The Prince of Wales has visited our town **twice.**
Princess Anne loves horses. I believe she goes riding **three** or **four times** a week.

Except in the case of *once* and *twice*, expressions of frequency are formed with the cardinal number + *times*.

34 Telling the time

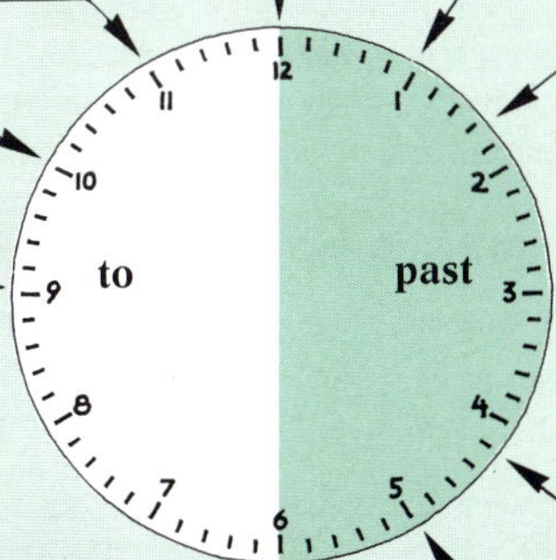

The full hour is referred to as *o'clock*. *Past* is used for times up to (and including) the half-hour **after** the full hour (*half past* ***twelve*** = *halb* ***eins***). *To* is used for times within the half-hour **before** the full hour (e. g. *quarter to one*).

It's **five** (minutes) past twelve.
It's **six minutes** past twelve.

The word *minutes* is usually left out with numbers that can be divided by 5 (5, 10, 15, etc.). In all other cases (i. e. numbers that cannot be divided by 5), *minutes* must be used.

N 1 It's 12.15 *(twelve fifteen)* – 8.30 *(eight thirty)* – 9.59 *(nine fifty-nine)*

In English as in German, it is also possible to give the hour first, and then the minutes *(twelve fifteen = zwölf Uhr fünfzehn)*. This is especially common when referring to very exact times (e. g. when reading or announcing train timetables or TV programmes).

N 2 Most of the shops open at 9 a.m. and close at 5.30 p.m. Only the supermarket stays open till 9 p.m.

To avoid misunderstandings, the times from midnight to noon can be given as *a. m.* [eɪ'em] (Latin *ante meridiem* = **before** noon), and the times from noon to midnight as *p. m.* [piː'em] (Latin *post meridiem* = **after** noon).

N 3 The plane will take off at **18.00** *(eighteen hours)*. It will land at **20.05** *(twenty-o* [əʊ]*-five)*.

The 24-hour clock is used particularly for air and rail travel times. In American English, 18.00 is often called *eighteen hundred hours* (BE eighteen hours).

§ 35 Prepositions in expressions of time

1. Times of day (exact and general)

at 6 o'clock – um 6 Uhr
at noon – um 12 Uhr mittags
at midnight – um Mitternacht

0 1 2 3 4 5 6 7 8 9 10 11 12 1 2 3 4 5 6 7 8 9 10 11 12

- 0–12: **in** the morning – am Morgen/Vormittag
- 12–5: **in** the afternoon – am Nachmittag
- 6–9: **in** the evening – am Abend
- 10–12: **in** the/**at** night – in der Nacht

Notice the difference:

in the morning, **in** the afternoon ◀ **period** of time (but: **at** night)

at 6 o'clock ◀ **point** in time

⚠ **on** the morning/evening ***of December 25th***, **(on)** ***that*** afternoon – refers to a **particular** morning/evening/afternoon

⚠ *Tonight* and *last night* correspond to German *heute abend* and *gestern abend.*

2. Days of the week, festivals and public holidays, months, seasons and years

Monday, Tuesday, Wednesday, Thursday, Friday, Saturday, Sunday

January, February, March, April, May, June, July, August, September, October, November, December

spring, summer, autumn (AE: fall), winter

in: **for months, years and seasons**

in January
in 1994 (im Jahr) 1994
in (the) spring, **in** (the) summer,
in (the) autumn/fall, **in** (the) winter
in the winter of 1985

at: **for festivals (Easter, Christmas)**

at Easter (time), **at** Christmas (time)

on: **for days of the week, days of the month, public holidays and other special days**

on Monday, **on** Tuesday, etc.
on the 12th of December
on my birthday, **on** Christmas Day, **on** Easter Sunday

No preposition before *next* and *last*

last Friday	(am) letzten Freitag
last January	(im) letzten Januar
next winter	(im) nächsten Winter

3. Other prepositions in expressions of time

We'll leave **after** breakfast.	*after*	nach
Try to be here **before** 9 o'clock.	*before*	vor
I met him two days **ago.**	*... ago*	vor (dem jetzigen Zeitpunkt)
I haven't seen her **since** 9 o'clock this morning.	*since*	seit (einem Zeitpunkt)
I haven't seen her **for** three hours.	*for*	seit (einem Zeitraum), (eine bestimmte Zeit) lang
The show starts sometime **between** 9 and 10 p.m.	*between*	zwischen
We watched TV **till/until** midnight.	*till/until*	bis
The programme will be on **from** 10 **to/till** 12 p.m.	*from ... to/till/until*	von ... bis
Could you please be ready **by** half past seven?	*by*	bis (spätestens)

36 Prepositions in expressions of place and direction

Prepositions which refer to position

by, near	the door
at	the table
under	the table
on	the table
over	the table
above	the bookshelf
below	the bookshelf
in front of/ before	the house
behind	the house
in	the house
outside	the house
against	the wall
round	the fire
opposite	the lady
among	his friends
between	her parents
beside	his mother

Prepositions which refer to direction

on, onto / **from, off**	the roof
over	the fence
towards / **to** / **into** / **out of** / **past**	the house
along / **across**	the road
after	the thieves
up / **down**	the hill
through / **round**	the trees

⚠ Notice the prepositions in the following expressions:

at the table	**am** Tisch	**in** the street	**auf** der Straße
on the wall	**an** der Wand	**in** the picture	**auf** dem Bild

N ***at/in*** **before the names of towns and villages:**

I live **in** London and my friend lives **in** Cardiff.

in: when the place is seen as an area (in which people live)

I don't think this train stops **at** York.

at: when the place is seen as a point (on a journey or route)

with/at **before (the names of) persons:**

Since his parents died he has been living **with** his aunt.
He always spends his summer holiday **at** his aunt**'s**.

bei seiner Tante (for permanent arrangements)
bei seiner Tante (for temporary arrangements)
(See § 8 for the use of the *s*-genitive here.)

into/in **to express direction:**

She went **into** the snackbar to have a cup of coffee.
She put lots of sugar **in** her coffee.

To express direction, *into* is normally used.
After *put,* however, *in* is more common.

Chapter 6: The adjective

37 Attributive and predicative use of adjectives

With most adjectives, two positions are possible:

	Adj.	**Noun**	
What a	**rough**	**match!**	The adjective can be placed before a noun (= attributive use).

	Verb	**Adj.**	
This match	**is**	**rough.**	The adjective can be placed after certain verbs, especially after *be* (= predicative use).

Adjectives used only predicatively

My friend is **ill.** ... ist krank.

But: The doctor examined the **sick** child.
... das kranke Kind.

The dog was **asleep** in front of the fire.

But: Let **sleeping** dogs lie.

We often went to Lincoln when Grandpa was still **alive.**

But: The characters in this book are not based in any way on **living** persons.

There's no danger. Don't be **afraid.**

But: Frightened animals sometimes attack unexpectedly.

David's parents were out, and he was **alone** in the house.
I don't need an alarm clock – I'm always **awake** at six thirty.

Some adjectives, such as *ill (= krank), asleep, alive, afraid, alone, awake,* can be used only predicatively, e.g. after the verb *be.*
There are often other adjectives with similar meaning, which can be used attributively (i.e. before a noun).

N the **only** chance — die einzige Chance
the **late** president — der verstorbene Präsident
a **late** visitor — ein später Gast — George was **late.** — George kam zu spät.

Some adjectives (e.g. *only*) cannot be used predicatively at all; others (e.g. *late*) cannot be used predicatively when they have a particular meaning.
Notice the difference in the meaning of *be sick* in British and American English:

He was **sick.** { BE: Er übergab sich.
AE: Er war krank.

§ 38 Adjectives after certain verbs

be, seem, keep, remain, stay

The party ***was*** **wonderful.**
The house ***seems*** so **empty** now without you all!
Please ***keep*** **quiet.** I'd like to listen to this record.

The verbs *be, seem, keep,* etc. refer to a state or quality (i.e. what something or someone is like). They are followed by an adjective.

become, get, grow, go, turn

You'll need a coat. It's ***becoming/getting*** quite **cool** in the mornings now.
It was ***growing*** **dark** as I started home across the fields.
He ***went*** **red** when the girl spoke to him.
Don't take Foxy's bone away – she might ***turn*** **nasty.**

The verbs *become, get, grow,* etc. are equivalents of German *werden.* They refer to a future state and are therefore also followed by an adjective.

look, taste, smell, sound

Those peaches in the window ***look*** **nice,** don't they?
The fish and chips ***smell*** **fantastic.** Let's hope they ***taste*** **good.**
'Upside down apple pie' – that ***sounds*** **interesting.**

The verbs *look, taste, smell* and *sound* can be used to refer to a quality (i.e. what something looks, smells, tastes or sounds like). In this case, they are followed by an adjective. (See note, however).

N It is also possible, however, to use the verbs *look, taste, smell, sound* for describing activities. In this case, they are followed by an adverb, not an adjective.

Quality: verb + adjective	**Activity: verb + adverb**
The soup ***tasted*** **awful.**	The cook ***tasted*** the soup **carefully.**
Die Suppe ***schmeckte*** **scheußlich.**	Der Koch ***probierte*** die Suppe **vorsichtig.**
Those little cakes ***look*** **delicious.**	She ***looked*** at the cakes **hungrily.**
... ***sehen*** **köstlich** ***aus.***	Sie ***sah*** die Törtchen **hungrig** ***an.***

§ 39 The comparison of adjectives

What you can say about things or people:

		comparative	*superlative*
a day:	**cold**	**- colder**	**- coldest**
a meal:	**big**	**- bigger**	**- biggest**
a poster:	**nice**	**- nicer**	**- nicest**
coffee:	**strong** [strɒŋ]	**- stronger** [ˈstrɒŋgə]	**- strongest** [ˈstrɒŋgɪst]
a trick:	**simple**	**- simpler**	**- simplest**
a boy/girl:	**clever**	**- cleverer**	**- cleverest**
a road:	**narrow**	**- narrower**	**- narrowest**
a joke:	**funny**	**- funnier**	**- funniest**

1. *-er, -est* are used to form comparatives and superlatives with:

   a) all adjectives of one syllable.

   Spelling: The final consonant is doubled after a short vowel. Final *-e* is left out.

   Pronunciation: After *-ng* [ŋ], an extra [g] is pronounced.

   b) adjectives of two syllables ending in *-le, -er, -ow* and *-y.*

   Spelling: *-y* is changed to *-i.*

a picture:	**beautiful**	**- more beautiful**	**- most beautiful**
a student in an exam:	**nervous**	**- more nervous**	**- most nervous**
a film star:	**famous**	**- more famous**	**- most famous**
an idea:	**good**	**- better**	**- best**
an accident:	**bad**	**- worse**	**- worst**
visitors:	**many**	**- more**	**- most**
money:	**much**	**- more**	**- most**
work:	**little**	**- less**	**- least**

2. *More/most* are used with:
   a) all adjectives of more than two syllables,
   b) most adjectives of two syllables that do not end in *-y, -le, -er* or *-ow.*

3. There are irregular comparative and superlative forms of: *good, bad* and the expressions of quantity *many, much, little.*

⚠ *Little = klein* has no comparative or superlative form. *Smaller – smallest* are used instead.

N 1 This programme about Alaska is **most** interesting. ... **höchst** interessant.

Most can also mean 'very', 'extremely'.

N 2 My **eldest** brother is five years **older** than my sister.

The forms *elder/eldest* are used before *brother, sister* and other members of a family, instead of the usual forms *older/oldest*. Before *than*, however, the usual form *older* is always used.

N 3 We could go to the Tower now. It's not **far** from here.
Buckingham Palace is much **further/farther** away. Please contact the tourist office for **further** information.

The comparative and superlative forms of *far* are *further/furthest*, or the less common forms *farther/farthest*. *Farther* is only used to refer to distances; *further* can be used for distances, but also to mean 'additional'.

⚠ Where is the **nearest** bus stop, please? – We must get off at the **next** stop.

Nearest means 'closest' (in distance), but *next* means 'following' (in a row or a series).

Notice the difference in meaning between *latest* and *last*:
her latest novel (= her newest/most recent novel) – *her last novel* (= the last novel she ever wrote).

0 Comparisons with adjectives

Comparisons are expressed in the following way:

Equal degree	Different degree
□ = □ **as** big **as** **as** important **as**	□ > □ bigg**er than** [ðən] **more** important **than**
New York is about **as big as** London. Sightseeing in Edinburgh can be **as exciting as** it is in London.	London buses are **bigger than** buses in New York. Living in a large modern city is **more dangerous than** living in the country.
	□ < □ **not as** big **as** (less common: **not so** big **as**)
	Cologne is **not as big as** London. (Cologne is **not so big as** London.) Most people would agree that Birmingham is **not as interesting as** London. (... **not so ... as**...)

⚠ The new car is much faster **than** my old one.
I'll take you out for a drive. **Then** you'll see what I mean.

Remember the difference between *than* and *then*.

N 1 Most people would agree that Birmingham is { **not as interesting as** / **less interesting than** } London.

Comparisons with *less ... than (weniger als)* have practically the same meaning as comparisons with *not as ... as*.

N 2 **The bigger** a city is, **the more difficult** it is to find one's way around.
Je größer ..., desto schwerer ...

The English construction with *the* + comparative ... *the* + comparative is the equivalent of German *je ... desto ...* .

N 3 **The High Street is the busiest** street in town. — **... die belebteste** Straße ...
The High Street is **(the) busiest** between 4 and 5 p. a. — **... am belebtesten ...**

The superlative is mostly used with *the*. But it can be used without an article when it corresponds to *am* + superlative in German.

§ 41 The use of the prop word *one/ones* with adjectives

One/ones to replace a noun already mentioned

Which of these **pullovers** do you like best? – The red **one** with the round neck. Den roten mit dem runden Halsausschnitt.
I've had these **winter boots** for ages. I really need some new **ones.** Ich brauche wirklich neue.

To avoid repeating a countable noun, the prop word *one/ones* is used in its place. A singular noun is replaced by *one*, a plural noun by *ones*.
Unlike in German, the adjective cannot be used alone.

'Perhaps I should have bought him a smaller one after all.'

N This **lamp**'s quite nice, but I think I prefer **the one** over there.
Look, this is **the one** I wanted to show you.
Let's decide on **this one** then. Or **which (one)** would you rather have?

The prop word *one/ones* is also used directly after *the, this, that* and *which*, to replace a countable noun.
It must be used after *the*, and is nearly always used after *this/that*.
After *which*, however, it can be left out.

42 Adjectives used as nouns

In English, unlike in German, adjectives can be used as nouns only in certain cases.

A whole class of people: *the* + adjective	Individual people: adjective + noun
The blind are usually educated at special schools. Die Blinden ... Years ago life was much more difficult for **the disabled** than it is now. ... für die Behinderten ... The BBC produce some good programmes for **the** very **young.** ...für die ganz Jungen.	**A blind man** stood at the side of the road with his guide dog. Ein Blinder ... Please don't make too much noise. Remember, there are **two sick people** in the next room. ... zwei Kranke ... **The little girl** looks very much like her mother. Die Kleine ...
An adjective used as a noun can refer only to a whole class of people: *the blind* = *blind people in general*, or *all blind people*. It has no plural *-s*, but it is used as a plural (e.g. *The blind* ***are*** ...).	To refer to individual people, it is necessary to add a noun such as *person, man, boy, girl, woman, people* to the adjective. Unlike in German, the adjective cannot be used alone.

N 1 There are a few **blacks** in our area, but they don't mix much with **the whites.**

There are a few adjectives which can be used as real nouns, and which take an *-s* in the plural.

N 2 The popular papers give a lot of emphasis to **the sensational.** ... betonen sehr das Sensationelle.
The good thing about our evening paper is that it gives all the local news. Das Gute an unserer Abendzeitung ist, ...

The + adjective can also be used to express a general abstract idea. If a particular case is referred to, however (here: *our evening paper*), a noun such as *thing* must be added to the adjective.

43 Adjectives and nouns expressing nationality

country	adjective	individuals	the people
America	an **American** car	an American	the Americans
Canada	a **Canadian** firm	a Canadian	the Canadians
Germany	a **German** stamp	a German	the Germans
Japan	a **Japanese** camera	a Japanese	the Japanese
China	a **Chinese** restaurant	a Chinese	the Chinese
Portugal	a **Portuguese** ship	a Portuguese	the Portuguese
England	an **English** pub	an Englishman/ an Englishwoman	the English
France	a **French** film	a Frenchman/ a Frenchwoman	the French
Spain	a **Spanish** dance	a Spaniard	the Spanish/ the Spaniards
Ireland	an **Irish** folksong	an Irishman/-woman	the Irish
Britain	a **British** plane	a Briton	the British

How to use them:

1. Adjectives ending in *-an* or *-ian* can also be used as nouns, with an *-s* in the plural.
2. Adjectives that end in *-ese*, when used as nouns, never take an *-s* in the plural.
3. Adjectives ending in *-ish* and *-ch* can be used as nouns only to refer to the nation as a whole, and are always used with an article, but without a plural *-s*. To refer to individual persons, compounds with *-man/-woman* are used, or in some cases special nouns (e.g. *a Briton*).

⚠ Compare the different spelling:

(in) **Britain** ['brɪtn] (in) Großbritannien (a) **Briton** ['brɪtn] (ein) Brite/(eine) Britin

Chapter 7: Adverbs and adverbial phrases

§ 44 Adverbs and adjectives

In German, adverbs and adjectives are often identical in form (e.g. *sie ist **vorsichtig*** – adjective; *sie fährt **vorsichtig*** – adverb). In English, however, different forms are used:

Adjective	Adverb ending in *-ly*
She is a **careful** driver. – She is very **careful.**	She drives **carefully**.
An adjective describes a quality (i.e. what a person or thing is like). Adjectives are used before nouns (attributive use) or after the verb *be* (predicative use). (See also § 37).	Here, the adverb is linked to the verb. It describes the way in which something is done.

'I thought it braked automatically.'

§ 45 The forms of the adverb

Adjective	Adverb
It was a **bad** accident.	Several people were **badly** injured.
The bus driver was **angry**.	He shouted at us **angrily**.
I've had a **terrible** day.	I'm **terribly** tired.
Dick told me the **whole** story.	It wasn't **wholly** his fault.
I shouldn't have got so angry, that's **true.**	I'm **truly** sorry about what happened.
Harry is sometimes very **rude.**	He spoke to me very **rudely** when I offered to help.
It was an **automatic** reaction.	He braked **automatically** when he saw the lorry on the wrong side of the road.
⚠ The police did a **good** job.	They did their job **well.**

1. Adverbs ending in *-ly*

Most adverbs are formed by adding *-ly* to the corresponding adjective.
Spelling and pronunciation:
- *-y* becomes *-ily* (exception: *shy/shyly*).
- *-le* after a consonant is left out.
- Final *-e* is left out in the case of *whole/wholly* and *true/truly*, but not otherwise.
- *-ic* becomes *-ically*.

The adjective *good* has an irregular adverb form: *well*.

Adjective	Adverb
It's a **fast** train. We had a very **long** journey. Sports cars always have **low** seats. Do you get a **daily** paper? We'll take the **early** train.	It travels very **fast.** The crossing didn't take **long.** That plane is flying very **low.** Our milk is delivered **daily.** We'll have to get up **early** to catch the train.
Please sign the form **here** and put it in that envelope **there.** Hasn't there been any post **today?** – No, but I expect the postman will be coming **soon.** I **often** used to get letters from Carol, but I **never** hear from her **now.**	

2. Adverbs with the same form as adjectives
These include:
- a number of adverbs of one syllable, such as *fast, long, low;*
- adverbs of frequency, such as *daily, weekly, monthly, yearly,* and the adverb of time *early.*

3. Adverbs with no corresponding adjectives
These 'original adverbs' include the adverbs of place *here* and *there*, adverbs of time such as *today, now, then, still, soon, yet*, and adverbs of frequency such as *often, sometimes, never.*

N Peter is such a **friendly** person. He smiled at me yesterday **in a very friendly way.**
It was a **difficult** climb. We only managed to get to the top **with great difficulty.**

Certain adjectives, e.g. *friendly, difficult*, cannot be used to form adverbs. Other expressions have to be used instead.

46 Double forms with different meanings

You've been practising very **hard** for Sports Day. – Yes, but I **hardly** think I'll have a chance against Paul in the 100 metres.	Du hast **hart** ... trainiert. ... ich glaube **kaum,** ...
Sue is good at tennis, I know, but she doesn't always play **fair.** She **fairly** often says balls were out when they were on the line.	..., aber sie spielt nicht immer **fair.** Sie sagt **ziemlich** oft, ...
I've **just** read that Smith has been dropped from the basketball team. In my opinion the decision was **justly** made.	Ich habe **gerade** gelesen, ... wurde die Entscheidung **zu Recht** getroffen.
You got back from the club very **late** again yesterday. Don't you think you've been spending rather too much time up there **lately?**	... sehr **spät** ... ... **in letzter Zeit** ...
Steve is **pretty** good at drawing and painting. Look how **prettily** he's done these Christmas cards.	... **ziemlich** gut ... ... wie **hübsch** ...

N Notice the difference here:

My father is not **well.**	Mein Vater ist nicht **gesund**. (Meinem Vater geht es nicht **gut.**)
He doesn't sleep **well.**	Er schläft nicht **gut**.

§ 47 Adverbs in comparisons

1. Comparative and superlative forms

Adverbs, like adjectives, form their comparatives and superlatives in three different ways (see also § 39):

How you can do things:

		comparative	*superlative*
work:	**hard**	**harder**	**hardest**
take notes:	**fast**	**faster**	**fastest**
speak:	**clearly**	**more clearly**	**most clearly**
look after your books:	**carefully**	**more carefully**	**most carefully**
use a dictionary:	**often**	**more often**	**most often**
speak a language:	**well**	**better**	**best**
write:	**badly**	**worse**	**worst**
talk:	**little**	**less**	**least**
enjoy reading:	very **much**	**more**	**most**

1. Adverbs of one syllable form their comparatives and superlatives with *-er/-est*.
2. *More/most* are used to form comparatives and superlatives with:
   a) adverbs ending in *-ly* (exception: *early/earlier/earliest)*
   b) other adverbs of more than one syllable.
3. There are irregular comparative and superlative forms of: *well, badly, little, much.*

2. Making comparisons with adverbs

Sally has only just passed her driving test, but she drives **as well as** Dad now.	... so gut wie ...
She certainly drives **faster than** Mum.	... schneller als ...
The InterCity gets to London **more quickly than** the other trains.	... schneller als ...
The buses here **don't** run **as regularly as** I thought.	... nicht so regelmäßig, wie ...

To make comparisons with adverbs, the same constructions are used as with adjectives. (See § 40).

N Did your mother cut your hair herself?
I must say, she's done it **most professionally.** ... sehr professionell ...

Most can also mean *very/extremely* (German *äußerst/höchst).*

'The buses here don't run as regularly as I thought.'

48 Adverbs of manner

Adverbs of manner describe the way in which something is done. They include most of the adverbs ending in *-ly* (see also § 44–45), and a number of adverbs without an ending, such as *fast* and *well*.

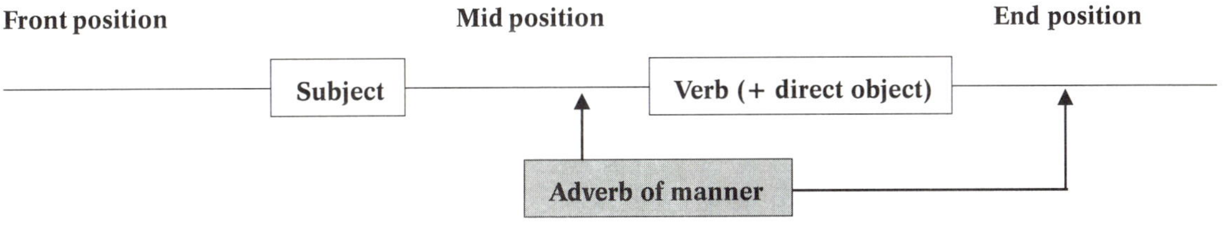

Sarah		changes her mind	**quickly.**
Sarah	**quickly**	changes her mind.	

Adverbs of manner usually appear in end position or in mid position.

End position: after the verb (+ direct object)	
Emma *talks* **quietly.** We all *listened* **carefully.** I thought Mark *read the poem* **beautifully.** He *acted his part* **well,** didn't he?	Adverbs of manner are placed immediately after the verb if it has no object. If the verb has a direct object, the adverb comes after that object.
Mid position: before the main verb	
Nancy **slowly** *began* to realize the truth. Now she *could* **easily** *imagine* why they hadn't given her the job. She *hadn't been* **fully** *accepted* as a candidate because she was black.	If the adverb is not stressed in the sentence (i.e. when it is less important in content than the rest of the sentence), it is placed in mid position, i.e. immediately before the main verb.

⚠ Compare English and German: Er nahm schnell das Geld.

He quickly took the money.

Unlike in German, adverbs of manner never come between the verb and the direct object.

49 Adverbs of degree

Adverbs of degree are used in order to make the meaning of another word stronger or weaker. They include adverbs ending in *-ly* such as *terribly, extremely, slightly,* as well as adverbs without an ending such as *very, pretty* (ziemlich), *much* and *quite*.

Position: before the adjective, adverb or verb to which they refer	
That was a **very** *good* idea. **Extremely** *clever,* in fact.	... eine sehr gute Idee. Außerordentlich klug ...
He got the answer **pretty** *quickly.*	... ziemlich schnell.
I find French **slightly** *easier* than German	... etwas leichter als Deutsch.
I **much** *prefer* maths to physics.	Ich mache viel lieber Mathe als Physik.
I **quite** *agree* with you.	Ich bin ganz deiner Meinung.

N He simply isn't *good* **enough** for the first team. — Er ist einfach nicht gut genug ...
He hasn't got **enough** *experience.* — Er hat nicht genug Erfahrung.

When it is used as an adverb, *enough* (like German *genug*) comes after the word it refers to. But if it is used as an expression of quantity, it comes before.

§ 50 Adverbs of indefinite time and frequency

Soon, never, sometimes, often, usually, mostly and *always* are among the most common adverbs of indefinite time and frequency.

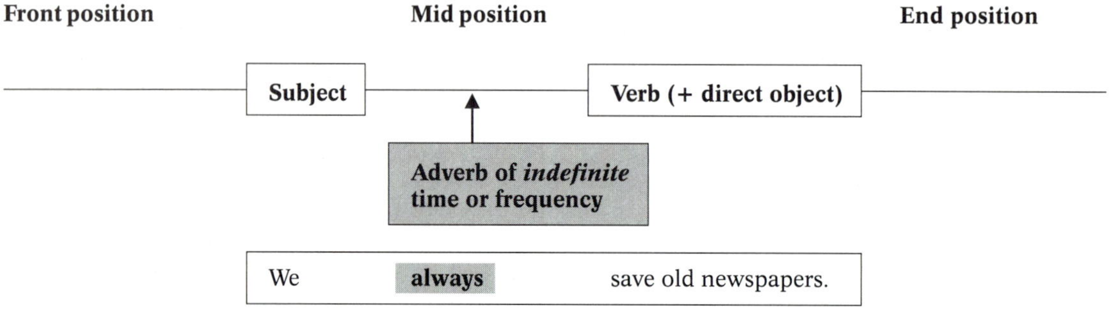

Adverbs of indefinite time and frequency are usually placed in mid position.

Position in sentences with a main verb only

People **often** *throw* their rubbish into the river here. — ... werfen ... oft ...
The water **never** *looks* very clean. — ... sieht nie sehr sauber aus.
But: The ducks *are* **usually** over there by the bridge. — ... sind gewöhnlich ...

If the sentence is formed with a main verb only (i.e. without an auxiliary), the adverb comes before the verb. **Exception:** If the main verb in the sentence is the verb *be*, the adverb comes after it (see third example).

Position in sentences with auxiliaries

There *has* **always** *been* a lot of traffic on this road.
The new housing estate *should* **never** *have been built* so near the motorway.

If the sentence contains an auxiliary, the adverb comes after it.
If there are several auxiliaries, the adverb comes after the first auxiliary.

N 1 **Sometimes** we leave the heating on at night. — We leave the heating on at night **sometimes.**
Soon alternative forms of energy will have to be found. — Alternative forms of energy will have to be found **soon.**

It is also possible to use front and end position with some adverbs of indefinite time and frequency (e.g. *soon, sometimes*).

N 2 **Hardly** had we moved into the house when we heard about the plans for the new airport. Kaum waren wir ...
Never (in my life) have I seen such an ugly building. Noch nie (im Leben) habe ich ...

In formal style, negative or restricting adverbs of indefinite time (e.g. *never, hardly)* sometimes appear in front position. This causes a change in the word order of subject and auxiliary (inversion). (See also § 149).

51 Adverbs of definite time and frequency

Today, tomorrow, yesterday are examples of adverbs of definite time. *Daily, weekly, monthly, once, twice* are examples of adverbs of definite frequency.

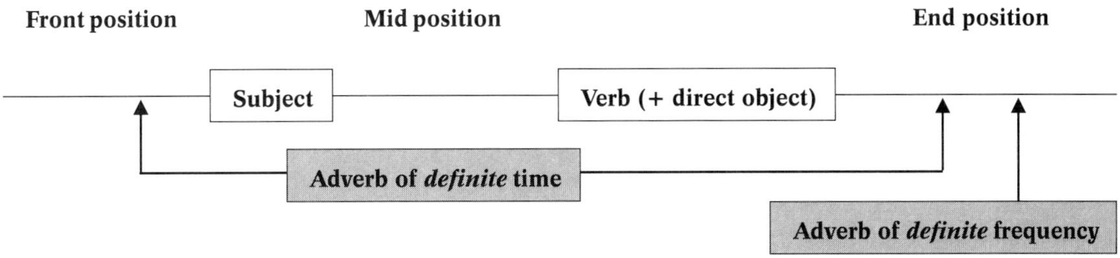

	We	watched a very interesting match	**yesterday.**
Yesterday	we	watched a very interesting match.	
	They	have won the World Cup	**twice.**

Adverbs of definite **time** appear in front position and in end position. Adverbs of definite **frequency** appear only in end position. Mid position is not used at all.

Definite time and frequency can also be expressed by adverbial phrases such as *last week, every day.* Like adverbs of definite time, these phrases appear in either front or end position (but never in mid position). (See also § 54).

52 Adverbs of place

The most common adverbs of place are: *here, there, upstairs, downstairs, inside, outside, somewhere, anywhere, everywhere.*

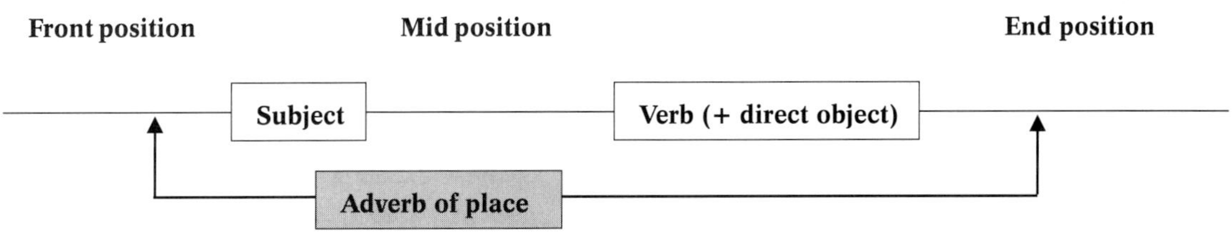

	They	sell sports equipment	**upstairs.**
Upstairs	they	sell sports equipment.	

Adverbs of place usually appear in end position, sometimes they appear in front position, but never in mid position.

Expressions of place usually consist of phrases such as *in London, at the station,* etc. Like adverbs of place, they take either end or front position, but never mid position. (See also § 54).

§ 53 Adverbs of comment

Adverbs of comment are used to make a comment on a whole sentence. They express the speaker's opinion. They include adverbs such as *luckily, (un)fortunately, of course, obviously.*

Front position		Mid position		End position
	Subject		Verb (+ direct object)	
Adverb of comment ↑				

Unfortunately	we	missed the early ferry.
Of course,	we	were able to take the later one.
Luckily	we	didn't have a rough crossing.

Adverbs of comment are usually placed in front position.

'Luckily I didn't book first class.'

N 1 Let's have lunch on the boat. Or we could go to a restaurant in Dover, **of course.**

Some adverbs of comment, especially *of course*, can appear in end position, as an extra comment or 'afterthought'.

N 2 The Dover Strait is the busiest shipping lane in the world. **Yet** one hears of surprisingly few accidents.

Front position is also usual with adverbs that link sentences together, such as *yet* and *however.* (See also § 145.)

54 Adverbial phrases

Groups of words such as *in London, last night, by car* are known as adverbial phrases. They have the same function as adverbs, and they usually refer to place, to definite time or frequency, or to means (e.g. to means of transport like *by car*, or to means of payment like *by cheque*).

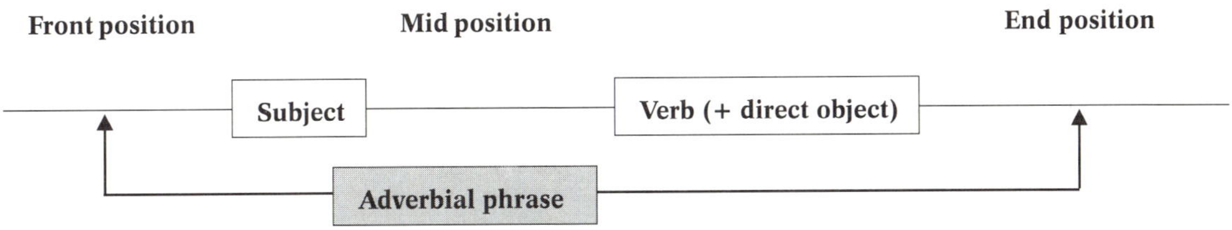

	My parents	bought a new car	**last year.**
Last year	my parents	bought a new car.	

I took my driving test **in Bristol.**
We made the whole journey **by coach.**
A few weeks ago my brother had a very bad accident **on the M25.**
Every weekend the trains to the Southwest seem to get more crowded.

Adverbial phrases usually appear in end position. Front position is possible, however, especially with adverbial phrases of time and frequency.
Adverbial phrases do not appear in mid position.

55 The order of different adverbials at the end of a sentence

Sometimes two or more different adverbs and adverbial phrases appear one after another at the end of a sentence.

Usual order: Manner – place – time

That new band played **well at the rock concert.**	**manner – place**
We left the cinema **quickly at the end of the film.**	**manner – time**
Elvis Presley first made rock popular **in America in the 1950s.**	**place – time**
The gospel choir sang **beautifully at our church last Sunday.**	**manner – place – time**

N He went **to London by car yesterday morning**. **place – means – time**

Adverbial phrases of means such as *by car* usually come between adverbials of place and time.

More exact time before more general time

I have to leave for school **at eight on weekdays**, but I stay in bed **until ten o'clock on Sundays.**

Chapter 8: The tenses of the verb

§ 56 The use of the simple and progressive forms: basic principles

simple form:

Mr Brown **works** as a reporter for the 'Gazette'.
(Mr Brown **works** = it is his job.)

progressive form:

Mr Brown **is working** on an article about comprehensive schools.
(Mr Brown **is working** = he is busy at the moment.)

progressive form

beginning not clearly stated → activity in progress → and not yet over

Each tense in English has a simple form and a progressive form (e. g. *he works:* simple form of the present tense, and *he is working:* progressive form of the present tense).
All verbs can be used in the simple form. But the progressive form is possible only with verbs that can describe an activity in progress or a gradual development.

Simple form	Progressive form	
My brother **reads** a lot of science fiction stories. I **walked** all the way home from school yesterday. After a long day's work everybody **gets** tired.	He **is reading** a book by Asimov at the moment. While I **was walking** home, it started to rain. Let's have a rest; **I'm getting** tired.	The progressive form is possible: – with verbs such as *read, walk, eat, work,* etc. (These verbs, which describe activities or events, can be called 'activity verbs'.) Most verbs belong to this group. – with verbs such as *become, grow, get (= werden).* (These verbs, which describe a development or a process of change, can be called 'process verbs'.)
Have you **noticed** that Lucy is wearing your shoes? I **don't see** my anorak anywhere. Do you **know** where it is? I **like** your new pullover. I **wish** I had one like it. That jacket **isn't** mine. It **belongs** to Barbara. Mum's new dress **looks** nice, doesn't it?		The progressive form is normally **not** possible: – with *notice, see, hear, feel,* etc. (verbs of perception). – with *know, believe, think, like, want, wish* and other verbs expressing knowledge, opinions, feelings or wishes. – with *be, have, contain (enthalten), possess (besitzen), belong* and other verbs expressing a state or a relationship such as owning or belonging; and with *seem (scheinen), mean (bedeuten), sound (klingen)* and *look (aussehen).*

N 1 Verbs that can be used in the progressive form are sometimes called *dynamic verbs* [daɪˈnæmɪk].
Verbs that cannot be used in the progressive form are sometimes called *stative verbs* [ˈstætɪv].

N 2 Some stative verbs, such as *be, think* and *have,* can also be used in the progressive form, but with a different (dynamic) meaning:

You **are** in a bad mood today. Du bist heute schlecht gelaunt.	You **are being** sarcastic. Du bist/verhältst dich ...
I **think** they live in Glasgow. Ich glaube/Ich bin der Meinung ...	We'**re thinking** of moving to Cambridge. Wir überlegen, ob ...
The house **has** two bathrooms. ... hat/verfügt über ...	Sarah **is having** a bath. ... badet/nimmt ein Bad.

57 The present tense: simple and progressive forms

1. Forms

Simple present	
I **like** tea. We **like** eggs. You **like** coffee. You **like** brown bread. He/She/It **likes** milk. They **like** chocolate.	The 3rd person singular ends in *-s*. All other persons, singular and plural, are identical to the infinitive in form.
She **speaks** [-s] English. It often **rains** [-z] in Ireland. He never **watches** [-ɪz] football.	Pronunciation and spelling of the 3rd person singular: – The *-s* is pronounced [s] after a voiceless consonant. Otherwise it is pronounced [z]. – After a sibilant [s, z, ʃ, ʒ, tʃ, dʒ], *-es* [ɪz] is added to the infinitive form *(watch – watches; freeze – freezes)*.
Mr Brown often **flies** to London.	– After a consonant, *-y* becomes *-ies (fly – flies; hurry – hurries)*.
⚠ Dad **does** [dʌz] the shopping. He **goes** [gəʊz] into town by bus. Mum **says** [sez] she needs the car.	Note the irregular forms *does* [dʌz], *goes* [gəʊz] and the irregular pronunciation of *says* [sez].
Present progressive	
I **am working.** We **are working.** You **are working.** You **are working.** He/She/It **is working.** They **are working.**	The present progressive is formed with *am/are/is* and the present participle (*-ing*-form).
We **are sitting** in the garden. The dog **is running** after the cat.	Spelling of the *-ing*-form: – After a short stressed vowel, the final consonant of the verb is doubled *(sit – sitting; run – running)*.
The sun **is shining.** Grandpa **is taking** the dog for a walk. The others **are lying** on the beach.	– Final *-e* is left out *(shine – shining; take – taking)*. – *-ie* becomes *-y (lie – lying; die – dying)*.

2. The use of the simple present

Simple present for facts that do not change
Dry wood **burns** well. Water **doesn't run** uphill. The M5 **joins** the M4 at Bristol. Holly **grows** wild in most parts of Britain. Lots of people in Wales **speak** Welsh.

The simple present is used for facts that do not change, e. g. laws of nature, qualities that are typical, and abilities.

Simple present for habits
My sister **takes** the dog out *every morning.* I *always* **cycle** to work. David *sometimes* **mows** Mrs Johnson's lawn for her. My parents *never* **go** into London by car.

The simple present is used to describe what someone regularly, seldom or never does. Sentences of this kind often contain expressions of frequency such as *always, often, sometimes, never, every morning.*

Simple present for a series of actions or events
...Brown **gets** the ball, **passes** it to Coker – and ... it's a goal! In 'Robinson Crusoe', Defoe **describes** how Crusoe **builds** himself a house on the desert island, **makes** a boat, and **meets** the native whom he later **names** Friday.

The simple present is also used to describe a series of actions or events that happen one after another. It is used especially in sports commentaries, in vivid narrative descriptions, and in summaries.

N Comments on texts are also written in the simple present.

Dad is watching the boat race.

3. The use of the present progressive

Present progressive for what is taking place at the moment of speaking
Dad **is watching** the boat race on TV at the moment. Right now they**'re going** under Hammersmith Bridge, and the Oxford crew **are leading.** But the Cambridge boat **is following** close behind.

The present progressive is normally used only with activity or process verbs (see also § 56).

It is used to describe activities or happenings which are taking place at the moment of speaking, and which are not yet over. It is often combined with adverbials of time such as *at the moment, right now,* etc.

Present progressive for what is going on over a longer period of time
Our local football team **is playing** very well this season. My uncle **is writing** a book about golf. **I'm doing** a lot of jogging these days.

The present progressive is also used for activities going on over a longer period of time (*this week, this season,* etc.), when they are seen as temporary. The activity need not be actually going on at the moment of speaking, but will be continued again later.

N You**'re always talking** about getting a new job, but you never do anything about it.
She**'s continually telling** me what to do.

Adverbs of frequency such as *always* and *continually* are sometimes used with the progressive form.
In this case, the speaker wishes to express an emotional attitude (such as anger or irritation) towards certain habits or repeated actions.
For neutral statements about frequency, however, the simple form is always used. (See § 57.2: Simple present for habits.)

58 The present perfect: simple and progressive forms

1. Forms

Simple present perfect

I	**have**	**arrived.**	We	**have**	**arrived.**
You	**have**	**arrived.**	You	**have**	**arrived.**
He/She/It	**has**	**arrived.**	They	**have**	**arrived.**
He	**has**	**gone.**	They	**have**	**come.**

Present perfect progressive

I/You	**have**	**been**	**waiting.**
He/She	**has**	**been**	**sleeping.**
It	**has**	**been**	**raining.**
We/You/They	**have**	**been**	**watching** TV.

The simple present perfect is formed with *have/ has* and the past participle.
Past participles can be divided into two groups:
- regular forms ending in *-ed* (spelling and pronunciation follow the same rules as past tense forms ending in *-ed:* see also § 60.1)
- irregular forms (see Appendix 1).

The present perfect progressive is formed with *have/has* + *been* + present participle (*-ing*-form). (See also § 57.1 – present progressive – for the spelling of the *-ing*-form)

2. The use of the simple present perfect

Effect or result is stressed

Clare **has hurt** her foot badly. Dad's at the hospital with her now.
Dr Benson **has gone** to London. I'm afraid you can't see him this week.
Don't touch those hot plates – **I've *just* taken** them out of the oven.
We **haven't received** the results of the blood tests ***yet,*** Mrs Taylor.
I've *never* taken sleeping pills.
Have you **had** your medicine ***yet,*** David?
Have you ***ever*** **been** to this hospital for treatment before?

The simple present perfect is used to stress the effect or result of a past action on the present.
It is also used

- for actions or events that have just been completed (sentences with *just*)
- for what has not happened yet (sentences with *not yet* and *never*)
- in questions about whether something has happened yet – or has ever happened (questions with *yet* and *ever*).

State lasting up to the present

Rachel is one of my oldest friends. **I've known** her for years. Ich kenne sie schon seit Jahren.
This is Miss Marks, our new assistant.
She**'s** only **been** here since September.
Sie ist erst seit September hier.
I don't know what's the matter with me.
I've felt tired all day.
Ich fühle mich schon den ganzen Tag müde.

With verbs that are not used in the progressive form (see § 56), the simple present perfect can express a state that began in the past and still continues. Sentences of this kind always contain an adverbial of time such as *since ..., for ..., all day long,* etc. (In German, the *Präsens* with *schon* is often used here.)

3. The use of the present perfect progressive

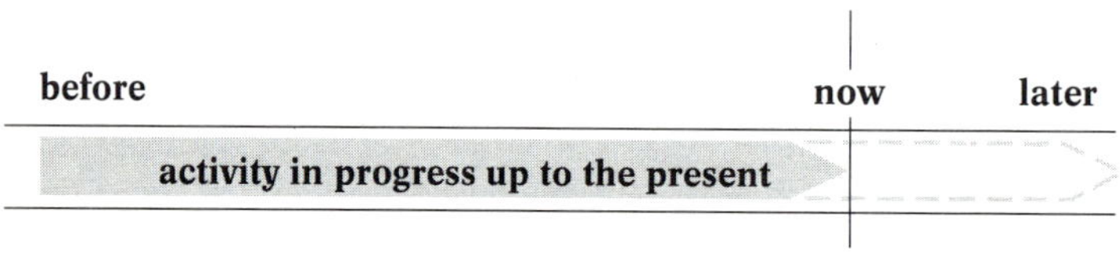

Present perfect progressive: Activity continues into the present

Switch the light off now. You**'ve been reading** ***for ages.*** ... Du liest schon ewig.
Dad **has been working** in the garden ***since lunch,*** and he's still busy. ... arbeitet schon seit ...
It**'s been raining** ***all day.*** I don't think it'll stop now. Es regnet schon den ganzen Tag.
Hurry up! We**'ve been waiting.**
Beeil dich! Wir warten schon.

The present perfect progressive is normally only used with activity and process verbs (see § 56). It is especially common with verbs such as *lie, sit, stand, wait, rain, shine* and *snow.*
It expresses the fact that something has been going on until now (and may still continue).
To state how long the activity has been going on, a time adverbial such as *since ..., for ...* is generally used. (In German, the *Präsens* with *schon* is often used.)

'Let's have a rest here. We've been travelling all day.'

N Dr Clarke and Dr Adkin { **have been working** / **have worked** } together for many years.

With activity verbs, it is sometimes possible to use the simple present perfect for activities that have been in progress up to now. However, the progressive form is usually preferred.

9 The use of *since* and *for* with the present perfect

since two o'clock: **point in time** when action or state began

for two hours: **period of time** for which action or state has continued

My brother has been working for British Rail **since 1986.** ... seit 1986 ... I've been trying to get a new job **since March.** The boss has been away **since Monday.** Jane has been living in London **since she started work at the BBC.**	Dad hasn't taken a holiday **for two years.** ... seit zwei Jahren/schon zwei Jahre lang ... Mike must be crazy. He's been sitting in front of that computer **for five hours** now. You ought to buy your own pocket calculator. You've been using mine **for ages.**
Expressions with *since* refer to the **point in time** when an activity or state began. *Since* is usually combined with an exact reference to time of day, date, day of the week, month, year, etc. (*since two o'clock, since 12th May, since Monday, since March, since 1986,* etc.). But *since* can also be used, as a conjunction, to introduce a subordinate clause (see example 4).	Expressions with *for* refer to the **period of time** for which an activity or state has so far continued. *For* is used in expressions such as *for two hours, for a few weeks,* etc. The time adverbials can also refer to inexact periods, e. g. *for weeks (schon seit Wochen), for ages (schon ewig).* *For* can also correspond to German *lang: zwei Jahre lang, fünf Stunden lang,* etc.

N I wasn't surprised to hear the news. I **had been expecting** it **for some time.** ...schon eine ganze Zeit lang ...
When I was a child, we **lived** in Munich **for about two years.** ... zwei Jahre lang ...
I'll be away **for at least two weeks.** ... mindestens zwei Wochen lang ...

Time adverbials introduced by *for* can be used in combination with other tenses as well as the present perfect. See also § 62.2 (top of page 63) for the use of *for* and *since* with the past perfect.

§ 60 The past tense: simple and progressive forms

1. Forms

Simple past

I/You/He/She/It/We/You/They { **arrived** early. / **came** early.

We **listened**	[-d]	to the radio.
They **liked**	[-t]	the concert.
It **ended**	[-ɪd]	at midnight.
She **cried**		at the end of the film.
He **stopped**		the video recorder.

There are regular and irregular past tense forms.

The regular forms end in *-ed*.
Pronunciation: [d] after a voiced sound,
[t] after a voiceless sound,
[ɪd] after [t] and [d].
Spelling:
– *-y* after a consonant becomes *-ie-*,
– after a short stressed vowel the final consonant is doubled.

See Appendix 1 for the irregular forms of the past tense.

Past progressive

I	**was**	**walking**	home.
You	**were**	**driving**	past.
He/She/It	**was**	**moving**	fast.
We/You/They	**were**	**waiting**	for the bus.

The past progressive is formed with *was/were* and the present participle (*-ing*-form).
See § 57.1. for the spelling of the *-ing*-form.

2. The use of the simple past

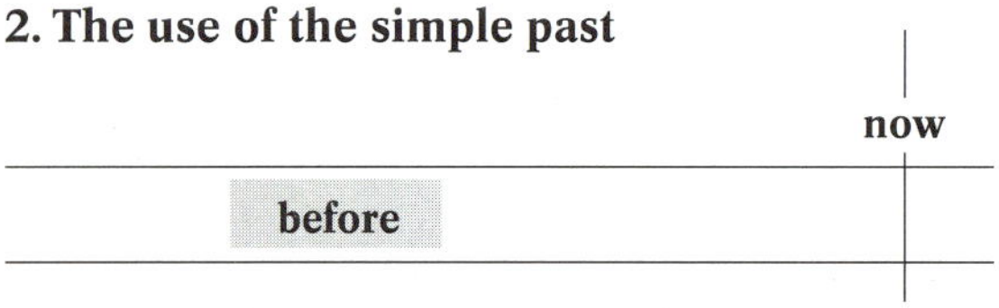

Simple past for past actions, events and states

We **went** to the theatre twice when we were in London *last week.*
Shakespeare **wrote** 'Romeo and Juliet' *some time in the 1590s.* He **died** *in 1616.*
When **did** you first **see** 'West Side Story'?
– I think it **was** *about three years ago.*

The simple past is used for completed actions, events and states in the past.
The time or period of time at which the action or event took place is often stated by time adverbials such as *yesterday, last week, three years ago, in 1960,* etc.
The simple past is used in questions with *when,* and in answers to these questions.

Simple past for a series of past actions or events

A gang of youths **appeared** at the corner. Sally **began** to walk away, but when they **saw** her, they **shouted,** and a moment later she **heard** the sound of running feet behind her.
The film **was** so silly that I **switched** off the TV set, **went** to bed and **read** my book for an hour.

The simple past is also used for descriptions of a series of past actions or events. For this reason it appears as a basic tense in stories (narrative texts) and reports about past events.

3. The use of the past progressive

before | now

activity in progress: past progressive

↑

new event: simple past

Past progressive for 'accompanying circumstances' (the 'background' to past events)	
We **were sitting** out in the garden when the thunderstorm *started.* Wir saßen gerade draußen im Garten, als ... While we **were taking** the chairs inside, the first drops of rain *fell.* Während wir gerade die Stühle hereinbrachten, ... Two children **were running** across the road in front of the school. The bus only just *stopped* in time.	An activity that was in progress (and not yet completed) when something 'new' happened, can be called the 'accompanying circumstances' (i. e. the 'background' to past events). The past progressive is used for the accompanying circumstances, and the simple past for the new event. The accompanying circumstances and the new event are often combined in one sentence with a main clause and a subordinate clause introduced by *when* or *while.*
Past progressive for several activities happening at the same time	
The baby **was crying** all the time while I **was talking** on the phone. There was a terrific noise in the house – the two dogs **were barking,** the children **were screaming,** and Peter **was shouting** at them all to be quiet.	If several activities were in progress at the same time, the progressive form is used for them all. Sentences with *while* are common here.

61 Past tense and present perfect in contrast

now

before: past tense

The past tense stresses that an action, event or state was **completed in the past.**

now

state or effect lasting up to now: present perfect

The present perfect stresses that an action, event or state began or happened in the past, but is **closely related to the present.**

Time adverbials that are used with the past tense: *yesterday, a month ago, last year,* etc., clauses with *when*	Time adverbials that are used with the present perfect: *since (Monday), for (two days), so far, (not) yet, already, ever/never (before/so far)*
Dad **flew** back from New York ***yesterday.*** The Clarks **went** to Australia ***last spring.*** We **took** hundreds of photos ***when we were on holiday.*** **Did** you **take** any pictures ***during the flight?***	The Smiths **have been** back home ***since Friday.*** We **haven't heard** from them ***since they went away.*** Aunt Sarah **has lived** in Sydney ***for ten years.*** – **Have** you ***ever*** **visited** her? – No, I **haven't had** a chance ***so far.*** ... bisher ...
Time adverbials of this kind refer to a point in time or a period of time that **belongs to the past** and is **now over.** For this reason, only the past tense is possible here.	Time adverbials of this kind refer to a period of time that began in the past, but **continues up to the present.** For this reason, the present perfect is used here.

'I've brought you a little souvenir.'

Present perfect to stress a result or effect in the present

We**'ve driven** nearly 500 miles today.
– No wonder you feel tired.
Would you like another cup of tea? – No, thanks. **I've had** enough.
Are there any more biscuits? – Sorry, Peter **has** just **taken** the last one.

The action or event is over, but its effect is still important. For this reason the present perfect is used.

N I **haven't been able** to go on holiday this year. (The year is not over yet: a holiday is still possible.)
I **wasn't able** to go on holiday this year. (The year is practically over: a holiday is no longer possible.)

Time adverbials such as *this week, this year,* etc. can be used with either the present perfect or the past tense, depending on what the speaker wishes to express.

§ 62 The past perfect: simple and progressive forms

1. Forms

Simple past perfect

I/You/He/She/It, We/You/They } **had arrived.**

The simple past perfect is formed with *had* and the past participle.
(See § 58 for the forms of the past participle.)

Past perfect progressive

I/You/He/She/It, We/You/They } **had been waiting.**

The past perfect progressive is formed with *had* + *been* + present participle (*-ing*-form).
(See § 57.1 for the spelling of the *-ing*-form.)

2. The use of the past perfect

then / at that time: past tense

before: past perfect

Simple past perfect for events or states that came before others in the past

The first pioneers *travelled* to California in 1849. Some of them **had emigrated** to the USA from Europe only a few months before.
After we **had visited** our relations in Toronto, we *flew* back to New York.

The past perfect is nearly always used together with past tense forms. The past tense describes what happened in the past ('then' or 'at that time'); and the past perfect describes what happened **further back in the past** ('before that time').

N The past perfect is especially common in reported speech (see also § 151).

then / at that time

activity or state continuing up to then

Past perfect for activities or states that lasted up to a certain point in the past

At last our flight to Manchester was announced. We **had been waiting** at the airport *since the early hours of the morning.*

The passengers knew nothing at all about the engine trouble, but the crew **had known** about it *for some time.*

In this sense, the past perfect is often combined with time adverbials introduced by *since* or *for.* If the continuation of an activity is stressed, the progressive form is used. With certain verbs, only the simple form is possible. (See § 56; see also § 58 for the use of the present perfect.)

63 Ways of expressing future time: table of forms and speech intentions

1. Forms

In English, future actions and events can be expressed in several different ways. The following forms can all refer to the future:

We're **going to travel** to London next week.	*going to*-future
We're **travelling** to London next week.	present progressive
We'll **be travelling** to London next week.	future progressive
We'll **take** the early train.	*will*-future
The train **leaves** at 7.30.	simple present

2. Speech intentions

The choice of form depends on speech intentions, i. e. on the aspect or point of view that the speaker wishes to stress. The most important speech intentions are shown in the table below. (See also §§ 64–69 for details and for other speech intentions.)

Plans and intentions:	*going to*-future	Barbara and I **are going to spend** a week in France next month.
Definite arrangements:	present progressive	My cousin **is travelling** with us. We**'re meeting** at Victoria Station.
Events that are naturally expected (as an understood thing):	future progressive	I suppose she and her mother **will be staying** the night at a hotel in London.
Predictions:	*will*-future	It **will take** us about an hour to get to Dover.
Fixed events (e.g. in official timetables):	simple present	Our train **leaves** at 10.15 a.m. When **does** the ferry **arrive** at Calais?

I'm going to collect the tickets tomorrow. Ich **hole** morgen die Fahrkarten ab.

Unlike the *Präsens* in German, the simple present is very rarely used for referring to the future.

§ 64 The *going to*-future

1. Forms

I	**am going to let**	the dog out.
He/She/It	**is going to play**	in the garden.
We/You/They	**are going to stay**	outside.

The *going to*-future is formed with *am/are/is + going to* and the infinitive. (The short forms of *be* are normally used. See § 82.2. and § 83.1.)

2. The use of the *going to*-future

Going to-future for plans and intentions

We**'re going to buy** Bobby a football for his birthday.
Are you **going to watch** 'Match of the Day' on TV tonight?
Judy says she**'s going to have** her own riding school *when she grows up.*

The *going to*-future is used to describe what someone plans or intends to do, mostly in the near future.

To refer to plans for the more distant future, corresponding time adverbials must be used.

Going to-future to express certainty

Look at those clouds. It**'s going to rain** soon.
We've still got a long way to cycle. We**'re going to get** wet, you can see that.

The *going to*-future can also be used when the speaker is sure that something will happen because there are already signs that it is inevitable (e.g. dark clouds which are a signal for coming rain).

§ 65 The *present progressive* to express future time

(See § 57.1 for forms.)

'We're leaving for Italy tomorrow morning.'

Present progressive for definite arrangements

Sorry, there's a terrible mess. We**'re leaving** for Italy *tomorrow morning.*
You needn't collect me *after the party.* **I'm coming** back with the Browns.

The present progressive describes definite arrangements that have been made for the future. A time adverbial (e.g. *tomorrow morning*) must be used to make it clear that the tense refers to the future and not the present; sometimes, however, this can be seen from the context. The present progressive is possible only with activity verbs (see also § 56).

6 The *will*-future

1. Forms

I/You/He/She/It We/You/They	**will** **'ll** **won't** [wəʊnt]	**start** tomorrow.
(I/We	**shall/shan't** [ʃɑːnt]	**start** tomorrow.)

The *will*-future is formed with *will* and the infinitive. In colloquial English, the short forms *'ll/won't* are normally used instead of *will/will not.*
(In British English, *shall/shan't* is sometimes used in the 1st person singular and plural.)

2. The use of the *will*-future

***Will*-future for predictions and suppositions**

Southern areas **will have** another bright day, but there **will be** a few showers in the North.
How old is Greg? – Sixteen. I think he**'ll be** seventeen next September. Yes, I'm sure he **will.**
I'm afraid I **won't be** here on your birthday.

The *will*-future is used to predict events over which the speaker has no control (e.g. the weather).
It is also used in subordinate clauses after certain verbs such as *think, be sure, be afraid.* (See also § 73 for the use of the *will*-future in conditional sentences.)

***Will*-future for spontaneous decisions and promises**

I've got to do the washing-up now, I'm afraid. –
I'll help you.

Will can also be used when the speaker suddenly makes a decision – or promises to do something – without having planned this before.

7 The future progressive

1. Forms

I/You/He/She/It/ We/You/They	**will** **'ll** **won't**	**be coming** tonight.
(I/We	**shall/shan't**	**be coming** tonight.)

The future progressive is formed with *will* + *be* + present participle.
(See § 57.1 for the spelling of the present participle, and § 66.1 for the use of *will* and the alternative form *shall.*)

2. The use of the future progressive

Future progressive for what is naturally expected to happen

You needn't phone Paul. We'**ll be meeting** him at the weekend, remember.
Shall I take my new cassette? – What for? We **won't be listening** to music this evening anyway.
I wonder what's happened to Janet and Brian. – Don't worry. I expect they'll **be arriving** soon.

The future progressive expresses what the speaker expects to happen 'naturally' (as an understood thing). It gives a neutral description of expected future events, whether they are planned or not.

N Julia **will be waiting** for us on the platform when the train arrives, I'm sure.

The future progressive can also describe an activity that will be in progress at a certain time in the future (here: the time when the train arrives).

§ 68 The simple present to express future time

Simple present in main clauses: for fixed events (e. g. in official timetables)

Hull – Brough – Goole – Doncaster – London

Sundays											
Hull	d	07 44	08 20	09 37	11 37	13 36	14 36	15 15	16 35	17 30	18 14
Brough	d	07 56	08 32	09 49	11 49	13 48	14 48	15 57	16 47	17 42	18 26
Goole	d	08 17	08 47	10 05	12 10	14 09	15 04	16 13	17 08	17 58	18 42
Doncaster	d	09 01	09 09	10 50	13 19	14 48	15 34	16 59	17 49	18 32	19 43
London (King's Cross)	a	12 27	13 00	13 50	15 40	17 10	18 00	18 55	20 00	20 27	21 35

Our train **leaves** at 2.36.
It **arrives** in London at six o'clock.
When **does** the concert **start**?

Unlike the present progressive, the simple present is used when future events have been decided on by an official 'authority'. It is often used to refer to exact times given in official timetables, programmes, etc.
The simple present is especially common with the verbs *arrive, leave, start* and *end.*

§ 69 The simple present in clauses of future time and in *if*-clauses

Subordinate clause: simple present – main clause: *will*-future

We'll ring you up *as soon as* we **get** there.
I'll send you a few photos *when* I **write** next.

If you **come** by air, we'll collect you at Heathrow.

In subordinate clauses of time which refer to the future (introduced by *when, as soon as,* etc.), the simple present is used, **not** the *will*-future. In the main clause, however, the *will*-future is used, not the simple present.

In conditional sentences (when they refer to a condition that can be fulfilled), the verb in the *if*-clause appears in the simple present; the verb in the main clause normally appears in the *will*-future. (See also § 73, 'Type 1'.)

N I'll play tennis with you as soon as **I've finished** my homework.

The present perfect is used in the subordinate clause to show that an action or event will be already completed at a certain time in the future.

0 The future perfect

1. Forms

I/You/He/She/It/ We/You/They { **will** / **'ll** / **won't** } **have gone.**

(I/We **shall/shan't** **have gone.**)

The future perfect is formed with *will* + *have* and the past participle. (See § 58.1 for the form and pronunciation of the past participle. See § 66.1 for the forms of *will* and the use of the alternative form *shall.*)

2. The use of the future perfect

Future perfect: Action or event will be completed by a certain time in the future

I'**ll have finished** my training by August.
Ich werde meine Ausbildung bis August abgeschlossen haben.
When you get back from London, we **will** already **have gone** on holiday.
Wenn du von London zurückkommst, werden wir schon in Urlaub gefahren sein.

The future perfect expresses the idea that an event or action will be already completed by a certain time in the future.
This point in future time can be mentioned in the form of a time adverbial such as *by August*, or in the form of a subordinate clause of time *(when ...).*

1 The conditional and the conditional perfect

1. Forms

I/You/He/She/It / We/You/They { **would** / **'d** } **come** today.

I/You/He/She/It / We/You/They { **would** / **'d** } **have come** today.

(I/We **should come** today.)
(I/We **should have come** today.)

The conditional is formed with *would* (short form: *'d*) and the infinitive.

The conditional perfect is formed with *would* (short form: *'d*) + *have* and the past participle.

(In the first person singular and plural, *should* is sometimes used instead of *would.*)

2. The use of the conditional and the conditional perfect

If I knew Susan's address, I **would send** her a card.

If I had seen you, I **would have told** you about the excursion.
Dad **would have collected** you if you had asked him.

In conditional sentences of the type in which a condition cannot be fulfilled, or can only theoretically be fulfilled, the conditional is used in the main clause. (See also § 73, 'Type 2'.)
When a condition can no longer be fulfilled, the conditional perfect is used in the main clause. (See § 73, 'Type 3'.)

He said he **would come** tomorrow.

They said they **would have moved** into their new house by the end of the month.

The conditional and the conditional perfect are often used in reported speech. They then correspond to the *will*-future and the future perfect in direct speech (see also § 151).

§ 72 The sequence of tenses between sentences

The two **basic tenses** in English are the present tense ('now') and the past tense ('then'/'at that time'). The use of all other tenses depends on which **basic tense** is chosen. This fundamental relationship is called the 'sequence of tenses'.

1. Present tense sequence (Basic tense = present tense: 'now')

Mike, 15, is talking about his interest in basketball.

before: past tense

now: present tense

later: *will*-future

up to now: present perfect

I **play** basketball. At the moment **I'm** in the second team.

My first match **was** about a year ago.

I've been practising twice a week for the last few months.

Our coach says **I'm making** good progress now.

Next year – with a bit of luck – **I'll be** in the first team.

When the present tense ('now') is the basic tense, it can be used in combination with the past tense, the present perfect and the *will*-future (or other forms of the future).
See §§ 57–61 and §§ 63–69 for details of the use of these tenses.

2. Past tense sequence (Basic tense = past tense: 'then'/'at that time')

Mike's mother remembers his interest in basketball as a twelve-year-old.

before that time: past perfect

then/at that time: past tense

later: conditional

up to then: past perfect

Mike **joined** the basketball club when he **was** twelve.

Even as a three-year-old he **had enjoyed** playing with balls.

He **had been playing** football for several years before he started basketball.

When he **became** a member, the coach at the club **told** me ...

... that he **would** soon **be** good enough to play in the junior team.

When the past tense ('then'/'at that time') is the basic tense, it can be used in combination with the past perfect and the conditional ('future-in-the-past').
See §§ 60, 62, 71 for details of the use of these tenses.

§ 73 The use of tenses in conditional sentences

In a conditional sentence, the *if*-clause (or 'conditional clause') expresses a condition, and the main clause expresses the result of this condition. There are three basic types of conditional sentences:

Type 1: Realistic conditions

Condition which can be fulfilled ***if*-clause: simple present**	– **Result in future time** **Main clause: *will*-future**
If you park your car there,	the neighbours **will complain.**
If I **don't see** Mrs Jones tomorrow,	**I'll ring** her up.

⚠ The *will*-future is never used in the *if*-clause, even when the condition refers to the future (as in *If I don't see Mrs Jones **tomorrow**, ...*).

N

If you **have sent** the letter off already,	you **can expect** an answer by the weekend.
If you **have had** enough to eat,	please **take** the things to the kitchen.

It is also possible to use other tenses (e.g. the present perfect) in the *if*-clause.

In the main clause, it is also possible to use the modal auxiliaries *can/may/must/needn't*, or to use an imperative.

Type 2: Theoretical conditions

'If I won ...'

Condition which cannot be fulfilled or is unlikely to be fulfilled ***if*-clause: past tense**	– **Theoretical result now or later** **Main clause: conditional (*would* + infinitive)**
If I **had** lots of money,	I **would go** on a world tour.
If we **spent** every winter in Spain,	we **would pick up** the language in no time.

The past tense form used in the *if*-clause does not actually refer to past time (as with *hatte, verbrachten*), but has the same meaning as a subjunctive form in German *(hätte, verbringen würden).*

⚠ The conditional is never used in the *if*-clause.

N

If you **came** back by plane,	we **could collect** you at Heathrow.

Instead of the conditional (i.e. *would* + infinitive), it is also possible to use *could (könnte)* + infinitive or *might (würde vielleicht)* + infinitive in the main clause.

Type 3: Theoretical conditions referring to the past

Condition which can no longer be fulfilled ***if*-clause: past perfect**	**– Theoretical result in past time** **Main clause: conditional perfect** **(*would have* + past participle)**
If I **had known** the exact time,	I **wouldn't have** missed my train.

The past perfect form in the *if*-clause, instead of having its usual meaning *(gewußt hatte)*, corresponds to a subjunctive form in German *(gewußt hätte)*.
⚠ The conditional perfect is never used in the *if*-clause.

N 1 The following combinations can also be used:

If you **didn't** always **drive** so fast,	you **would have seen** that sign.
Wenn du nicht ... fahren würdest,	hättest du ... gesehen.
If we **had left** home at eight this morning,	we **would be** in Scotland by now.
Wenn wir ... weggefahren wären,	wären wir jetzt schon ...

N 2 **Had I known** there was an emergency, I would have called the police at once.

The construction *Had I* + past participle is sometimes used in formal style instead of the usual *If I had* + past participle. (In this construction, *if* is left out, and the word order of subject and auxiliary is changed.)

74 The use of *were* und *was* in *if*-clauses

***If I/he/she/it were ...* - wenn ich/er/sie/es ... wäre**

If I **were** you,	I **wouldn't call** the police.
If there **were/was** any real danger,	it **would be** different, of course.
If your father **were/was** more polite to the neighbours,	there **wouldn't be** all this trouble now.

The verb *be* has a subjunctive form: *I were, he/she/it were*.
This form can be used in theoretical conditions (§ 73, Type 2).
In colloquial English, however, it has become common to use the indicative form *I was, he/she/it was*.

75 *Should* in *if*-clauses

If you **should get** lost,	you'**ll be** able to ask someone the way.
Wenn ihr euch verlaufen solltet,	...
If you **should be** in our area,	**ring** up and **let** us know.
If I **should be** out,	Peter **would answer** the phone and take a message.

Like *sollte* in German, *should* expresses a possibility.
The main clause in this case can be formed with the *will*-future, an imperative, or the conditional.

N

Should this door **be** closed,	please **use** the main entrance on the west side.
Sollte diese Tür geschlossen sein,	...

Like *sollte* in German, *should* can also introduce a subordinate clause expressing a condition.

§ 76 Past tense and past perfect to express wishes

***I wish/I'd rather/If only/It's (high) time* + past tense**	
I wish I **were/was** a millionaire.	Ich wünschte, ich wäre Millionär.
If only I **had** enough money for a trip to America.	Wenn ich doch nur genug Geld ... hätte.
I'd rather you **didn't spend** so much money on records.	Es wäre mir lieber, wenn du nicht soviel Geld für Schallplatten ausgeben würdest.
It's high time your parents **gave** you a bit more pocket money.	Es ist höchste Zeit, daß deine Eltern dir etwas mehr Taschengeld geben.

Here, the past tense does not refer to past time, but expresses a wish that cannot be – or is unlikely to be – fulfilled. (See also § 73, Type 2 for similar use of the past tense in theoretical conditions.)
Instead of *I was, he/she/it was,* it is common to use *I were, he/she/it were* (see also § 74).
In German, the corresponding phrases are followed by subjunctive forms (*wäre, hätte,* etc.), except in the case of *it's (high) time ... – es ist (höchste) Zeit, daß ...*

***I wish/I'd rather/If only* + past perfect**	
I wish I **had done** my homework.	Ich wünschte, ich hätte meine Hausaufgaben gemacht.
If only I **hadn't eaten** so much!	Wenn ich nur nicht so viel gegessen hätte.

Here, the past perfect expresses wishes that can no longer be fulfilled, since they refer to what happened in the past. (See also § 73 Type 3 for the past perfect in theoretical conditions referring to the past.)

Chapter 9: The passive voice – tenses and sentence patterns

The car is checked regularly.

77 The passive forms of the verb

1. Forms

Simple forms

The car **is checked** regularly.
It **was taken** to the garage yesterday.
The tank **has been filled** up.
The car **had been washed** before we left.
The new models **will be delivered** next week.
A car like this **would be sold** quickly.
The work **will have been done** by this evening.
The repairs **would have been finished** sooner if we hadn't been so busy.

In the simple form, all tenses of the active voice can also be formed in the passive:

present tense:	*am/is/are*	+ past participle
past tense:	*was/were*	
present perfect:	*have/has been*	
past perfect:	*had been*	
will-future:	*will be*	
conditional:	*would be*	
future perfect:	*will have been*	
conditional perfect:	*would have been*	

The car **must be washed.**
... muß gewaschen werden.
The rear light **should have been replaced.**
... hätte ersetzt werden sollen.

can, *must*, *should*, etc. + *be* + past participle (passive form of the infinitive) / *have been* + past participle (passive form of the perfect infinitive)

Progressive forms

My bike **is being repaired** at the moment.
My bike **was being repaired,** so I went by bus.

The progressive form is normally only used in the present and past tense. It is formed with:
am/are/is being / *was/were being* + past participle

(For the past participle, see § 58.1.)

1 He **got** badly **hurt** in the accident. — Er wurde ... schwer verletzt.
Don't leave your bike outside. It might **get stolen**. — ... Es könnte ... gestohlen werden.

In colloquial English, a construction formed with *get* + past participle is sometimes used as an alternative to the passive. The '*get*-passive' is especially used to express that an event is unintended or unexpected.

2 He wants **to be left** in peace. — For the passive forms of the infinitive, see also § 100.
He hates **being woken** up early. — For the passive forms of the gerund, see § 112.

2. The use of the passive in the simple form

The use of tenses is the same in the passive as in the active voice.

Examples	Explanation
The dustbins **are emptied** every Monday. Rubbish **is** never **collected** at the weekend.	The simple present is used when something is regularly, often, rarely, or never done. (See also § 57.2.)
The lawn **has been cut,** I see. It looks much better now. **Have** all the apples **been picked?**	The present perfect emphasizes the effect of a past event on the present. (See also § 58.2.)
Several big trees **were blown** down in a bad storm last autumn. Luckily nobody **was injured.**	The simple past stresses that an event in the past is over, and is not seen in connection with the present. (See also § 60.2 and § 61.)

N The gate **is locked** at 7 p.m. every evening. Das Tor **wird** jeden Abend um 7 Uhr **geschlossen.** (Here a process is described.)
We can't get in – the gate **is locked.** ... – das Tor **ist geschlossen.** (Here a state is described.)

In the simple form of the present and past, the passive can be used to describe a state as well as a process. (In German, two different auxiliaries – *werden* and *sein* – are used for these two different 'types' of passive.)

'Our TV is being repaired at the moment.'

3. The use of the passive in the progressive form

Examples	Explanation
Have you heard? The cinema in Station Road **is being turned** into a disco. Two new houses **are being built** in our road at the moment.	The present progressive is used to describe what is happening at the present time (at the actual moment of speaking), and not yet completed. (See also § 57.3.)
When I walked past yesterday, the windows **were being put** in.	The past progressive is used to describe what was in progress at a particular time in the past. (See also § 60.3.)

78 Passive sentences with and without a *by*-agent

	Subject		Object
Active:	The police	arrested	the thief.
	The thief	was arrested.	
Passive:	**Subject**		

Passive sentences can be formed with nearly all verbs that take an object in the active.
The subject of the passive sentence corresponds to the object of the active sentence.

Every day millions of telephone calls **are made.** New telephone books **are printed** regularly and **provided** free for all telephone users.
Hundreds of telephone boxes **were damaged** in the London area last year. Windows **were broken,** wires **pulled out** and telephone books **torn up.**

Very often, the agent (i.e. the person or thing that causes the action) is not mentioned in a passive sentence. This is especially the case when the agent or 'doer' is unimportant, obvious, or unknown.

	Subject		**Object**
Active:	Inspector Brown	arrested	the thief.
Passive:	The thief	was arrested	by Inspector Brown.
	Subject		***by*-agent**

Forest fires **are** often **started *by careless picnickers.***
The fire in the tower block **was** first **reported *by a passing taxi-driver.***
A 92-year-old woman, who was asleep in her 11th floor flat, **was** finally **rescued** from the flames ***by the fire brigade.***
Hundreds of fine old buildings **were destroyed *by the Great Fire of London*** in 1666.

The person or thing that causes the action can be mentioned in the form of a *by*-agent. Passive sentences of this kind are used particularly when it is important to emphasize who or what causes the action or event.

§ 79 Verbs with prepositions in passive sentences

	Subject	**Verb + preposition**	**Prepositional object**
Active:	Our friends	looked after	the children.
Passive:	The children	were looked after	by our friends.
	Subject	**Verb + preposition**	***by*-agent**

Our new neighbours don't seem very friendly.

They only speak if they**'re spoken to.**	..., wenn man sie anspricht.
Last night two houses in our road **were broken into.**	Heute nacht wurde in ... eingebrochen.
Since the afternoon of July 6th, 8-year-old Sarah Armstrong **has not been heard of.**	Seit ... hat man nichts von ... gehört.

Here the subject of the passive sentence corresponds to the prepositional object of the active sentence. The preposition is so closely linked to the verb that it remains in the same position in the passive. Sentences of this kind often correspond to active sentences with 'man' in German.

§ 80 Verbs with two objects in passive sentences

In the case of verbs such as *give, offer, send, hand, show* (see § 97.1), passive sentences can be formed in two different ways.

			Indirect object	**Direct object**
Active:	They	gave	the children	the best seats.

Passive: (1)

The children	were given the best seats.
Subject	

(2)

The best seats	were given **to** the children.
Subject	

Passive (1)	**Passive (2)**
We **were offered** a choice of five different kinds of ice-cream. Man bot uns ... an. My mother **has been sent** an enormous box of chocolates. Jemand hat ... geschickt.	The menu **has been handed to** the people sitting at the next table. Coffee **was given** only **to** the grown-ups (not to the children).
Here the subject of the passive sentence corresponds to the indirect object of the active sentence. As this is, in most cases, a person, the construction is called the 'personal passive'. Of the two passive constructions, it is the more common. When translating into German, it is often best to use sentences with 'man' or 'jemand'.	Here the subject of the passive sentence corresponds to the direct object of the active sentence (mostly a thing). The indirect object (mostly a person) is linked to the verb with *to*. This passive construction is normally only used when the indirect object is particularly long, or particularly stressed.

⚠ The dangers of leaving the group and riding over the moors alone **were explained to** us before the trip.

Passive sentences with verbs that always take an indirect object with *to* (e.g. *explain s.th. to s.o.*, see § 97.2) can only be formed with construction (2); i.e. only the direct object of the active sentence can be used as the subject of the passive sentence.

Cycling is said to be the most strenuous of all sports.

1 Passive sentences with verbs of saying and thinking

Cycling **is said to be** the most strenuous of all sports.

Compare: People **say** that cycling **is** the most strenuous of all sports.

Man sagt, daß Radfahren der anstrengendste Sport sei.

Team games **are supposed to be** good for us – but I much prefer athletics. ...sollen angeblich ...
The game of football **is thought to have started** in the 13th century. ... hat vermutlich ... begonnen.

The passive forms of verbs of saying and thinking (e.g. *say, believe, think, suppose, report*) can be followed by an infinitive construction. Sentences of this kind correspond to active sentences introduced by expressions such as *People say that ...*
In German they can be expressed with a *daß*-clause.

It is also possible in German to use constructions with the verb *sollen* or with adverbs such as *angeblich* or *vermutlich*.

Chapter 10: The auxiliaries

§ 82 Auxiliaries and main verbs (full verbs)

Most verbs are main verbs; only a small number are auxiliaries.
These include:
– *be, have, do* (which can also be used as main verbs; see § 83–85),
– the modal auxiliaries (*can, must, may,* etc.; see § 86).

1. The use of auxiliaries and main verbs in affirmative and negative statements and in questions

In affirmative statements

He		**speaks** **Main verb**	five languages.
He	**can** **Auxiliary**	**speak** **Main verb**	five languages.
He	**has** **Auxiliary**	**learnt** **Main verb**	five languages.

In affirmative statements, only main verbs can stand alone.

Auxiliaries, however, can be used only in combination with main verbs.

In negative statements

You	**needn't** **Auxiliary + *not***	**speak** **Main verb**	French.
She	**doesn't** **Auxiliary + *not***	**speak** **Main verb**	English.

Negative statements with *not* always include an auxiliary. *Not* (or the short form *n't*) is added to the auxiliary. If there is no other auxiliary in the sentence, *do* is used in this function. (See also § 138.)

In questions

Have **Auxiliary**	**you** **Subject**	**read** **Main verb**	the book?
Do **Auxiliary**	**you** **Subject**	**read** **Main verb**	a lot?

In questions, only an auxiliary can be used before the subject; a main verb can never take this position.
Do is used as an auxiliary if there is no other auxiliary in the sentence. (See also § 140.)

2. The long and short forms of auxiliaries

Auxiliaries, unlike main verbs, have short as well as long forms (see the tables of forms in § 83–86), e.g. *I'll help you.* = *I **will** help you; I **can't** come.* = *I **cannot** come.*

Informal style: short forms	Formal style: long forms
I'm afraid I **can't** come to Bristol this weekend. **We'll** let you know when we**'ve** booked our flight. You**'re** coming back on Sunday, **aren't** you?	We **are** very sorry that Lady Fitzgerald **cannot** be here with us today. Unfortunately I **have not** received a reply to my letter of April 21st.
In colloquial English (including informal letters to friends, etc.), the short forms of the auxiliaries are normally used.	The long forms are generally used only in formal style (in public speaking, in business letters, essays, etc.).

N **I can** [kən] swim. **Can** [kæn] *you swim?* – Yes, I **can.** [kæn]
I must [məs(t)] go. **Must** [mʌst] *you go?* – Yes, I **must.** [mʌst]

Can and *must* have no short forms, but they are normally pronounced with a weak vowel sound [ə].
In *yes/no* questions and short answers, however, *can* and *must* are pronounced with the full vowel sound.
Similarly, the short forms of *is* and *will* cannot be used in *yes/no* questions or short answers.
Compare: *It'll be too late.* But: ***Will*** *it be too late? – Yes, it* ***will****.*

3 *Be* used as an auxiliary and as a main verb

1. Forms

Present tense			Past tense	
Long forms	**Short forms**		**Long forms**	**Short forms**
I **am** **(not)**	I' **m** **(not)**		I **was** **(not)**	I **wasn't**
you **are** **(not)**	you' **re** **(not)**	you **aren't**	you **were** **(not)**	you **weren't**
he / she / it **is** **(not)**	he' **s** / she' **s** / it' **s** **(not)**	he / she / it **isn't**	he / she / it **was** **(not)**	he / she / it **wasn't**
we / you / they **are** **(not)**	we' **re** / you' **re** / they' **re** **(not)**	we / you / they **aren't**	we / you / they **were** **(not)**	we / you / they **weren't**
Non-finite verb forms: Infinitive: **be**	*-ing*-form: **being**		Past participle: **been**	

1 **Aren't I** clever? I'm getting in your way, **aren't I?**

In questions and question tags, *aren't I* is normally used instead of *am I not.*

2 In pop songs and other original texts, the non-standard dialect form *I ain't/ain't I* [eɪnt] is sometimes used instead of *I'm not/aren't I.*
(The form *ain't* is also sometimes used instead of *isn't, haven't/hasn't.*)

2. The use of the verb *be*

The auxiliary *be:* as part of the progressive form and of the passive	
Please be quiet! Mark and I ***are* listening** to the news. Can I have the paper now? You**'ve *been* reading** it for ages.	The forms of *be* are used together with the present participle to form the progressive form.
The western we saw last night ***was* filmed** in Spain. 'Oliver Twist' **has *been* shown** at least three times. I don't want to watch it again.	They are used together with the past participle to form the passive. (See also § 77.)
The main verb *be*: as a linking verb	
The Hunters **are** both doctors. Peter's grandfather **is** very ill, I believe. The hospital **is** on the other side of York. Visiting hours **are** from 4 pm to 6 pm.	As a main verb, *be* is always used to link the subject of the sentence with a noun, an adjective, or an adverb of place or time. It expresses a state, a quality, or some other kind of relationship.
Is the surgery still open? The instructions say that these travel pills **are not** suitable for small children.	In this function, *be* always appears in the simple form. Questions and negative statements are always formed without *do*.
Where**'s** Mrs Tate? She **isn't** in the waiting-room.	The short forms can always be used, even when *be* has the function of a main verb.

N You **are being** very difficult today. Du bist (= verhältst dich) heute sehr schwierig.

The main verb *be* can be used to refer to someone's behaviour at a certain moment. In this sense, it appears in the progressive form.

§ 84 *Have* used as an auxiliary and as a main verb

1. Forms

Present tense				Past tense			
Long forms		**Short forms**		**Long forms**		**Short forms**	
I, you	**have (not)**	I've, you've **(not)**	I, you **haven't**	I, you, he, she, it, we, you, they	**had (not)**	I'd, you'd, he'd, she'd, it'd, we'd, you'd, they'd **(not)**	I, you, he, she, it, we, you, they **hadn't**
he, she, it	**has (not)**	he's, she's, it's **(not)**	he, she, it **hasn't**				
we, you, they	**have (not)**	we've, you've, they've **(not)**	we, you, they **haven't**				
Non-finite verb forms:	Infinitive: **have**		*ing*-form: **having**		Past participle: **had**		

⚠ The short forms *'s* and *'d* can stand for *is* and *would*, as well as for *has* and *had*. Notice the difference:

He**'s** — (= he **is**) going home. / (= he **has**) gone home.

He**'d** — (= he **would**) go home. / (= he **had**) gone home.

2. The use of the verb *have*

The auxiliary *have:* as part of the perfect tenses

Judy **has left** school now.
I **would have done** better in my exams if I **had worked** harder.

When used together with the past participle of a main verb, the forms of *have* produce the perfect tenses (present perfect: see § 58; past perfect: see § 62).

Alan **hasn't taken** his A-levels yet.
Have you **finished** your English essay already? That was quick!

As with all auxiliaries, questions and negative statements with *have* are formed without *do*.

The main verb *have*: questions and negative statements formed with *do*

As a main verb, *have* can be used in a number of different meanings.

One of my uncles **has** a farm in Scotland.
John and his brother both **have** very dark hair.
Your grandmother **had** small hands just like yours.

Like the German verb *haben*, it can be used to mean 'possess'. In this sense, it can appear only in the simple form.

My great–grandparents **had** seven daughters, but they **didn't have** any sons.
Did they **have** a big house? – Yes, they **did**.

Negative statements and questions are generally formed with *do* (if no other auxiliary is used). (See N 2, however.)

Have a good time at the weekend!
We **were having breakfast** when they arrived.
Wir frühstückten gerade ...

There are also a large number of idiomatic verbal expressions formed with *have* + noun. Because these expressions describe activities, *have* can appear in the progressive form here.

Do you always **have a walk** after lunch on Sundays?
I **didn't have a bath** last night, I **had a shower.**

When *have* is used as part of such a verbal expression, questions and negative statements must always be formed with *do* (if no other auxiliary is used).

1 See § 90 for *have to* meaning *must*.
See § 124 for *have something done* (*have* + noun + past participle) in the sense of 'cause an action to be done by someone else'.

2 **Have** you **(got)** any brothers and sisters?
– Yes, I **have (got)** a sister, but I **haven't (got)** any brothers.

When used in the sense of 'possess', *have* in the present tense need not take *do* in questions and negative statements. In colloquial (British) English, *have got* is generally preferred; it is used in the present tense only, and never takes *do* in questions and negatives.

"Bye, Jane. Have a good time!'

5 *Do* used as an auxiliary and as a main verb

1. Forms

		Long forms	Short forms	Non-finite verb forms
Present tense	I/you he/she/it we/you/they	**do (not)** **does (not)** [dʌz] **do (not)**	**don't** **doesn't** ['dʌznt] **don't**	Infinitive: **do** *-ing*-form: **doing** Past participle: **done**
Past tense	I/you/he/she/it we/you/they	**did (not)**	**didn't**	

2. The use of the verb *do*

The auxiliary *do*: in questions and negative statements

Do you like jazz? – Yes, I **do**, but I **don't** like this band very much.
Ann plays the guitar, **doesn't** she?
– Yes, she **does**, and so **do** I.

That blond girl **did** sing beautifully!

When a sentence contains no other auxiliary, *do* is used
- to form questions and negative statements (see also § 138 and § 140),
- in question tags, short answers, and short sentences with *so, nor, neither* (see also §§ 142–144),
- to add extra emphasis to a statement (see also § 148).

The main verb *do*

What's Gill **doing**? – She's **doing** her French homework.

What **do** you **do** in your free time? – I go swimming a lot in the summer, but I **don't do** much in the winter.

As a main verb, *do* is an activity verb; it is often used in the progressive form.

The auxiliary *do* is used to form questions and negative statements when *do* is used as a main verb (in sentences with no other auxiliary).

§ 86 The modal auxiliaries

1. The most common forms

Present tense forms			Past tense forms		
Affirmative forms (long and short)	**Negative forms (long and short)**		**Affirmative forms (long and short)**	**Negative forms (long and short)**	
can	cannot	can't [kɑ:nt]	could	could not	couldn't
may	may not		might	might not	mightn't
must	must not	mustn't ['mʌsnt]			
need	need not	needn't			
will 'll	will not	won't [wəʊnt]	would 'd	would not	wouldn't
shall	shall not	shan't [ʃɑ:nt]	should	should not	shouldn't
			ought to	ought not to	oughtn't to

N See § 92 and § 94 **N** for the less common auxiliaries *used to* and *dare.*

2. Differences between modal auxiliaries and main verbs

Always with the infinitive

My brother **can speak** Spanish.
May I **borrow** your dictionary?

You **ought to learn** your French words.

English: I **must go** home now.
German: Ich **muß** jetzt nach Hause (gehen).

Modal auxiliaries always appear together with the infinitive of a main verb. The infinitive is used without *to.*
(Exceptions: *ought to, used to.*)

In English, unlike in German, it is not possible to leave out the infinitive (except in short answers and other short sentences, e.g. *Yes, I must; So must I*).

No *-s* in the 3rd person singular

Bob **can** drive now.
Where's the car? – It **must** be in the garage.

The present tense forms have no *-s* in the 3rd person singular (i.e. with *he, she, it*).

Missing forms – substitutes

You **can't** go to school with a temperature. But I expect you**'ll be able to** go back on Monday.
I really **must** go to bed. I feel terrible.
We **had to** call the doctor in the middle of the night.

The modal auxiliaries exist only in either one or two tenses (mostly present tense and past tense – see 1: 'The most commmon forms'). Substitutes, formed with verbs of similar meaning, are used for the missing forms of the other tenses.

The use of the past tense forms

Could you tell me the way to the harbour, please? Könnten Sie mir bitte sagen ...?
Would you please drive a bit more slowly here? We **might** miss the turning. Würdest du bitte hier etwas langsamer fahren? Wir könnten ... verpassen.

The past tense forms do not usually refer to the past; they mostly correspond to German subjunctive forms (*könnte, würde,* etc.).
(See § 88, 91, 92 for past tense forms which do refer to the past.)

Constructions such as *should have done*

We **should have got up** earlier. I can see that now. Wir hätten früher aufstehen sollen.
You **needn't have collected** me at the airport, I **could** easily **have taken** a taxi.

When referring to the past, an auxiliary is often followed by the perfect infinitive of a main verb (*have* + past participle). This construction corresponds to a subjunctive construction in German (*hätte ... sollen,* etc.).

37 Modal auxiliaries and speech intentions

You may ... *You mustn't ...* *You can ...* *You must ...*

Modal auxiliaries are very often used to express a wish or a personal attitude to something.
Some typical speech intentions:

- making a request
- asking for, giving or refusing permission

- telling someone not to do s.th.
- explaining that something is necessary or not necessary
- giving advice
- expressing a criticism
- expressing what one supposes:

Something is thought to be
  - certain
  - probable
  - possible

Will/Would/Can/Could you do me a favour?
Can/Could/May/Might I use your telephone?
You **can/may** come in now.
Can/May I go now? – No, you **can't/may not**.
You **mustn't** wake the baby.
You **must** tell me the truth.
You **needn't** wash up today. I'll do it.
You **should/ought to** take an extra pullover.
You **shouldn't/oughtn't to** go to bed so late.

There's someone at the door. – It **must** be the postman.
The phone's ringing again. – It**'ll** be John.
Sue wasn't at work today. She **may/might/could** be ill.

§ 88 *Can/could*

To express ability: *can/can't, could/couldn't* **Substitute form: *be able to***		
Present tense	I **can** understand French when it's spoken slowly, but I **can't** understand Spanish at all. Ich kann Französisch verstehen, ..., aber ich kann überhaupt kein Spanisch verstehen.	Like *können* in German, the auxiliary *can* is used to express ability. (Negative form: *cannot/can't.)*
Past tense	We **couldn't** understand what the policeman said. Wir konnten nicht verstehen, ...	The past tense forms of *can* are *could* and *couldn't*.
Other tenses	Ellen **has been able to** speak Italian since she was a small child. Ellen kann seit ihrer Kindheit Italienisch sprechen.	For other tenses, *be able to* is used as a substitute.

N I don't speak much Greek, but I'**m able to** explain what I want most of the time.
..., aber ich kann meistens erklären / es gelingt mir meistens, zu erklären, ...
The banks were closed, but we **were able to** change some money at the hotel.
..., aber wir konnten etwas Geld im Hotel wechseln.

Be able to can also be used in the present tense and in the past tense. In these cases, it is normally used in the sense of 'succeed in' or 'manage to'.

To make a request: *Can ...?/Could ...?* **To give (or to refuse) permission: *can/can't***	
Can/Could you lend me five pounds? Kannst/Könntest du mir fünf Pfund leihen? **Can/Could** I park the car here? – No, I'm afraid you **can't**. Kann/Könnte ich den Wagen hier parken?	Questions with *can* and *could* are used – to ask someone to do something, – to ask for permission.
You **can** use the telephone over there. You **can't** sit at this table, madam. It's reserved.	*Can* and *can't* are also used to give – or to refuse – permission.
I don't think we'**ll be allowed to** take the dog into the hotel dining-room. Ich glaube nicht, daß wir den Hund mit in den Speisesaal nehmen dürfen.	For other tenses (when referring to permission), *be allowed to* is used as a substitute. (See also § 89.)

N 1 I'm not sure whether we're going the right way. – Well, we **could** ask that policeman over there.

Could can also be used to make a suggestion.

N 2 Surely this **can't** be the way to the beach?

Can't is sometimes used as a way of saying, 'I don't think it is possible ...'.

89 *May/might/mustn't*

To ask for and to give permission: *may* To refuse permission or to forbid: *may not, mustn't*	**Substitute form: *be allowed to***
Present tense	**May** I borrow your biro? – Yes, of course you **may**. Darf ich ...? You **may** use a dictionary for this exercise. Ihr dürft ... ein Wörterbuch benutzen. Martin Berry has got a pet alligator. **May** I have one too? – No, you certainly **may not**. Nein, das darfst du auf keinen Fall. You **mustn't** give a dog chicken bones. Man darf einem Hund keine Hühnerknochen geben.
Other tenses	In Oliver Cromwell's time, people **weren't** even **allowed to** play cards. ... durfte man nicht einmal Karten spielen. Women **have been allowed to** vote in Britain since 1918. We'**ll be allowed to** listen to a discussion in the House of Commons, but we **won't be allowed to** talk to the Prime Minister, of course.

May is used to ask for permission and to give permission (so especially in questions and in answers to these questions). (In requests, *might* can be used to express extra politeness: ***Might** I ask you a question?*)

May not is practically only used in short answers, i.e. to refuse permission when someone has asked for it.

In other cases (i.e. when explaining that something is forbidden or 'against the rules'), *mustn't* is preferred.

In the past tense and in all other tenses, *be allowed to* is used as a substitute.

1 Only buses **are allowed to** drive along the High Street now. — Nur noch Busse dürfen jetzt ... fahren.
Are we **allowed to** park on this side of the road?
We're going by train after all. John **isn't allowed to** take his parents' car.

It is also possible to use *be allowed to* in the present tense.

2 He **may** be ill. He **might** even be in hospital. — Er ist **vielleicht** krank. Er **könnte** sogar im Krankenhaus sein.
He **may not/might not** have got our letter. — Er hat unseren Brief **vielleicht nicht** bekommen.

May/might (have) are very often used to express that something is possibly the case. *Might* suggests less probability than *may*.
The negative forms *may not/might not (have)* express that something is possibly **not** the case.

90 *Must/needn't*

To express a necessity or duty: *must* Substitute form: *have to*	
Present tense	We **must** leave now. We haven't much time before the last bus goes. Wir müssen jetzt gehen. You **must** come and visit us again soon. It's always lovely to see you. Ihr müßt uns bald wieder besuchen.

Must is used
- when one thinks something is necessary,
- to instruct or encourage someone to do something.

Must appears only as a present tense form.

Other tenses	There was a railway strike, so we **had to** go to Birmingham by coach. ..., deshalb mußten wir mit dem Bus ... fahren. **Did** you **have to** book seats on the train? The main road to Whitby was closed because of an accident, so we **were forced to** use the coast road. The Wilsons aren't usually late. **I've** never **had to** wait for them before. If we should miss the last bus, we**'d have to** walk three or four miles home.	For the past tense, substitute forms are used. *Had to* is the most common. Questions are formed with *did ... have to*, negatives with *didn't have to*. Other substitute forms: *was/were forced to, was/were obliged to*. For other tenses, *have to* is also the most common substitute form.

N 1 Most people **have to** get up early on weekdays. — Die meisten Leute müssen ... früh aufstehen.
When **have** you **got to** leave tomorrow? — Wann mußt du morgen weggehen?

It is also possible to use *have to* in the present tense. *Have got to* is an alternative form; it appears only in the present tense, however.

N 2 It's five o'clock – the match **must** be nearly over.
Listen to the noise – our team **must** have won.

Here, *must* expresses that there are good reasons to suppose that something is the case: it is practically certain. In this sense, *have to* cannot be used.

To express that something is unnecessary: *needn't* Substitute form: *not + have to*		
Present tense	You **needn't** take me home. I can get a bus. Du brauchst mich nicht heimzubringen. It's lucky that I **needn't** cycle to school in this rain.	*Needn't* is used when one thinks that something is not necessary. It appears only as a present tense form.
Other tenses	We went into a first class compartment, but we **didn't have to pay** extra. ..., aber wir brauchten nicht extra zu bezahlen. Why don't you take the ferry from Harwich? Then you **wouldn't have to** drive all the way to Dover.	For the past tense, *didn't have to* is the usual substitute form. *Have to* is also generally used to form the other tenses.

⚠ Compare English and German:
You must = *Du mußt*
You mustn't = *Du darfst nicht*
You needn't = *Du mußt nicht/ Du brauchst nicht*

The answer to the question *Must I ...?* is either *Yes, you must* or *No, you needn't*.

N See § 94 for *need* as a main verb.

'You mustn't climb up there. It's dangerous.'

'You needn't walk up the stairs, madam. There's a lift over there.'

1 *Will/would* and verbs corresponding to German *wollen*

To express or to request willingness: *will/would*

Will you set the table while I'm making the salad? Würdest du den Tisch decken, ...?
Would you help me with the cooking today, please? Würdest du mir heute beim Kochen helfen?

Will you/Would you is used to ask if someone is willing to do something. It forms a request. *Would* shows extra politeness.

Don't worry about supper for me. **I'll** make myself a sandwich when I get back. ... Ich mache mir ein belegtes Brot, ...

I'll (or *we'll*) expresses one's own (and others') willingness to do something. (See also § 66.)

Dinner at the Royal would be pretty expensive. I don't know whether Dad **is prepared to** pay that much. Ich weiß nicht, ob Papa bereit ist, ...
John's parents **were willing to** take us to the dance in their car. Johns Eltern waren bereit, ...

In the 3rd person (singular and plural), and in other tenses, willingness can be expressed with *be willing to* or *be prepared to.*

To express a wish: *would like to, want to*

I'd like to get a job again this summer. Ich würde gern ... eine Arbeit annehmen.
What **would** you **like to** do? Was möchtest du tun?
Would you **like to** work in my uncle's office? I'm sure he **would like to** give you a job.

Would like to (short forms: *I'd like to/he'd like to,* etc.) can be used to express a wish, or to ask about others' wishes.
Questions with *would you like to* are often invitations or offers.

Philip **wants to** sit in the front row.
Do you **wish to** collect the tickets before the show? Wünschen Sie, die Karten ... abzuholen?
We **wanted to** get to the theatre in good time. Wir wollten rechtzeitig ins Theater kommen.
I **have** always **wanted to** see a Broadway musical.

Want to, or the less common form *wish to,* can also be used to refer to wishes. *Want* and *wish* can appear in all tenses, and are therefore used to refer, for example, to past wishes.

It is more polite to use *I'd like to .../Would you like to ...?* than it is to use *I want to/Do you want to ...? I wish to* and *Do you wish to ...?* are formal in tone.

To express refusal: *won't, wouldn't*

John has asked me to lend him my cassettes, but I **won't**. ..., aber das werde ich nicht tun.

I wanted to borrow my sister's walkman, but she **wouldn't** let me have it. ..., aber sie wollte ihn mir nicht geben.

Won't and *wouldn't* are used to show that someone is or was determined not to do something. *Won't* refers to both the present and the future. *Wouldn't* here is used as a genuine past tense form, meaning 'refused to' or 'was not willing to'.

My parents **have** always **refused to** buy a video recorder. They say we all watch too much TV anyway. Meine Eltern wollten nie ... kaufen.
Alan **will** never **be prepared to** lend you his new camera. You know what he's like! Alan wird bestimmt nicht bereit sein, dir ... zu leihen.

For other tenses, forms of *refuse to* – or the negative forms of *be prepared to, be willing to, want to* – are used.

Where's Jack? – He'**ll** be in the garden. I expect he **will** have planted the roses by now.
Er wird im Garten sein. Er wird wohl inzwischen die Rosen gepflanzt haben.

Will can also be used to express what one supposes is very probable.

§ 92 *Used to*

'That's strange. There used to be a bridge here ...'

To express past states and habits: *used to* + infinitive
There **used to** be a shoe factory on that side of the road. **Früher** war auf der anderen Straßenseite eine Schuhfabrik. My sister and I **used to** walk past it on our way to school. Meine Schwester und ich gingen ... **immer** daran vorbei. In those days, Southfield Park **used to** be a girls' grammar school. Damals war Southfield Park ein Gymnasium für Mädchen.

Used to appears only in the past tense; it has no present tense form.
In German, a verb form in the past + *früher* or *immer* often corresponds to *used to* + infinitive.
Used to is not always translated, however.

N 1 Life **used not to** be easy a hundred years ago.
People **didn't use to** have much free time.
Most people **never used to** have a holiday.

There are several different negative forms of *used to*, e.g. *used not to, didn't use to, never used to*.

N 2 My great-grandfather **would** get up at five o'clock every morning.
Mein Urgroßvater stand (gewöhnlich) jeden Morgen um fünf Uhr auf.

A past habit can also be expressed with *would*. Unlike *used to*, however, *would* is only used with verbs that can describe repeated activities.

§ 93 *Shall/should/ought to/be to* corresponding to German *sollen*

To make a suggestion: *Shall I ...? Shall we ...?*
Shall I make the sandwiches? **Shall we** put the drinks in this basket?

Shall I ...?/Shall we ...? can be used to make a suggestion, or to ask someone else if a suggestion is acceptable.

To give advice, to express criticism: *should/ ought to*

You **shouldn't** drink so much coffee, you know.
John really **ought to** leave some of those super cheese sandwiches for the rest of us.

Should and *ought to* both correspond to *sollte (eigentlich)* in German.

Have an egg. Oh dear, we **should have** remembered to pack salt and pepper.
I **shouldn't have** eaten so much – but everything tasted so delicious!

The forms *should have/ought to have* + past participle correspond to German *hätte sollen.* They express criticism of what has been done wrong – or not done at all.

To refer to instructions given (or arrangements made) by someone else: *be to*

Can you lend me your list of youth hostels? **I am to** make the reservations for the whole group.
Ich soll (Ich habe den Auftrag) ...
I've just talked to the warden on the phone. We**'re to** bring our own sleeping bags, as they don't provide them at the hostel.

Be to is used to express what someone else has instructed or ordered.

The coach **was to** leave at nine o'clock, but we didn't actually set off till half past. Der Bus sollte um neun Uhr abfahren (es war so vereinbart), ...

A plan already arranged by someone else can also be expressed with *be to.*

'You see, we ought to have taken the motorway.'

1 New York **is supposed to/is said to** be one of the most exciting cities in the world.

Be supposed to and *be said to* are used in the sense of German *soll angeblich.* (See also § 81.)

2 It's best that the girls **should** share the double room on the first floor.
Es ist am besten, wenn die Mädchen das Doppelzimmer im ersten Stock teilen.
How strange that the Hayletts **should** have booked at our hotel.
Wie seltsam, daß Hayletts in unserem Hotel gebucht haben.

Should can sometimes appear in *that*-clauses after expressions giving a personal opinion (e.g. *It's best, How strange, I'm sorry/surprised).* It has no equivalent in German, and so is left untranslated.

§ 94 *Need* and *dare* used as auxiliaries and as main verbs

1. *Need*

***Need* as an auxiliary: only in questions and negative statements**	***Need* as a main verb: in all sentence types**
Need I fill in this form? Tell Paul he **needn't** write a letter. He can ring up instead. The waiting-room is empty. We **needn't have** made an appointment. ... Wir hätten uns nicht anzumelden brauchen.	**Do** we **need to** finish all this today? A lot of work still **needs to** be done. There was plenty of time, so we **didn't need to** hurry. ..., deshalb brauchten wir uns nicht zu beeilen.
As an auxiliary, *need* appears **only** in questions and negative statements. Remember also: – Questions and negatives are formed **without *do***. – There is **no *-s*** in the 3rd person singular. – The infinitive that follows appears **without *to***. – The only forms are *need/needn't* (followed by the infinitive or the perfect infinitive, e.g. *need (not) have done*).	As a main verb, *need* can appear in affirmative statements as well as in negative statements and questions. Remember also: – Questions and negatives are formed **with *do***. – The 3rd person singular ends in ***-s***. – The infinitive that follows appears **with *to***. – *Need* as a main verb can appear in **all** tenses.

2. *Dare*

***Dare* as an auxiliary: only in questions and negative statements**	***Dare* as a main verb: mainly in questions and negative statements**
I **daren't** ski down here – look how icy it is! We had planned to climb all the way to the top, but in the end **none** of us **dared** go on. **How dare you** camp in this field?	**Did** you actually **dare to** walk onto the tennis court in the middle of the match? I'd love to have a game with Christine, but she plays so well, I **wouldn't dare to** ask her. The new coach isn't very good, but **nobody dares to** say so.
As an auxiliary, *dare* appears **only** in negative statements and questions (especially with *how ...?*). There is also a past tense form, *dared*, although this is less common than the present tense form. Otherwise, *dare* is used according to the same rules as *need* as an auxiliary (see above for questions and negatives, etc.).	As a main verb, *dare* appears **mainly** in negative statements and questions (but never in questions with *how ...?*). Otherwise, *dare* as a main verb is used according to the same rules as *need* as a main verb (see above for the use of *do*, etc.).

Chapter 11: The verb and its objects and complements

5 Verbs without an object and verbs with an object

Subject	Verb
He	**was reading.**

Subject	Verb	Object
He	**was reading**	**a book.**

Most English verbs can be used either without an object (intransitive use) or with an object (transitive use). *Read, write, eat,* etc. are typical examples. Whether they are used with or without an object, their meaning remains the same.
This is not the case, however, with the following verbs:

Similar in form but different in meaning: verbs such as *lie – liegen/lay – legen*	
Verb without an object	**Verb with an object**
After lunch Dad **lay** on the sofa for half an hour. Nach dem Mittagessen lag Papa ... auf dem Sofa.	**He laid** *his hand* on my shoulder. Er legte mir die Hand auf die Schulter.
Forms: **lie** [laɪ] – **lay** [leɪ] – **lain** [leɪn] *(liegen)*	Forms: **lay** [leɪ] – **laid** [leɪd] – **laid** *(legen)*
Mrs Jacobs **rose** to meet us when we entered the room. ... erhob sich...	He **raised** *his glass* and wished us a happy New Year. Er erhob sein Glas ...
Forms: **rise** [raɪz] – **rose** [rəʊz] – **risen** ['rɪzn] *(sich erheben)*	Forms: **raise** [reɪz] – **raised** [reɪzd] – **raised** *(etw. erheben)*
May I **sit** here? Or is this seat reserved? Darf ich mich hier hinsetzen?	You've got to get up early tomorrow, so don't forget to **set** *your alarm clock*. Vergiß nicht, deinen Wecker zu stellen.
Forms: **sit – sat – sat** *(sitzen, sich setzen)*	Forms: **set – set – set** *(etw. setzen, stellen)*
What's all that noise? – Little Johnny has **fallen** off the sofa. ... ist vom Sofa gefallen.	Our view down to the river is much better now that they've **felled** *those big trees*. ..., seit sie diese großen Bäume gefällt haben.
Forms: **fall – fell – fallen** *(fallen)*	Forms: **fell – felled – felled** *(fällen)*
Identical in form but different in meaning: verbs such as *grow, run, work*	
Verb without an object (intransitive use: 'doing s.th.')	**Verb with an object (transitive use: 'causing s.th. to happen')**
Tomatoes **grow** well in the Channel Islands. ... wachsen ... gut. We'll catch the bus all right if we **run**. ... wenn wir laufen. I'm afraid the cassette-recorder you lent me doesn't **work**. Der Kassettenrecorder ... funktioniert leider nicht.	Our neighbours **grow** *a lot of vegetables* in their garden. ... bauen viel Gemüse an(‚lassen es wachsen'). My uncle **runs** *a big holiday camp*. ... leitet ein großes Feriencamp (‚sorgt dafür, daß es funktioniert'). I hear you've got a new computer. Can you **work it** yet? Kannst du ihn schon bedienen (‚zum Funktionieren bringen')?

N I've **put** your magazines on the table over there. — Ich habe deine Zeitschriften auf den Tisch ... **gelegt.**
Lunch is ready. – I'll **put** baby Jo in her highchair. — ... – Ich **setze** Klein-Jo in ihren Hochstuhl.
Could you **put** those wine glasses in the cupboard? — Könntest du diese Weingläser in den Schrank **stellen**?

The English verb *put* is much more common than *lay* or *set*. It can be used in nearly all cases where *legen, setzen* or *stellen* would be used in German.

§ 96 Phrasal verbs

Subject	Verb	Preposition	Object
She	**looked**	**at**	her watch.

Subject	Verb	Particle	Object
She	**took**	**off**	her coat.

Verbs that are used in set combinations with either a preposition (*at, to, into,* etc.) or an adverbial particle (*off, up, away,* etc.) are known as 'phrasal verbs'.

Set combination: verb + preposition or adverbial particle

Dad stopped at the side of the road and **looked at** the map.	... schaute ... an.
Where are the car keys? Peter's **looking for** them.	... sucht ...
Barbara **looked after** the cat while we were away.	... kümmerte sich um ...
I'm really **looking forward to** our trip to Scotland.	Ich freue mich ... auf ...
The plane is **taking off**.	... startet.
Travelling **takes up** a lot of my father's time.	... nimmt ... in Anspruch.
John **takes after** his grandfather in many ways.	... ähnelt/schlägt ... nach ...
Mum has **taken on** a lot of extra work recently.	... hat ... übernommen.
Where's Sally? – She's **taking** the papers **round.**	... trägt ... aus.

Many verbs can be used in set combinations with a number of different prepositions or adverbial particles. In each case, the meaning is different.

Further examples of common phrasal verbs:

get in	einsteigen (in)	*put on*	anziehen
get off	aussteigen (aus)	*put out*	löschen (Feuer)
get on with	zurechtkommen mit	*put through*	verbinden (am Telefon)
get over	hinwegkommen über		
give away	verschenken	*put off*	verschieben
give up	aufgeben	*put up*	aufstellen
look out for	Ausschau halten nach	*put up with*	sich abfinden mit
look up	nachschlagen (im Lexikon)	*ring up*	anrufen
		take along	mitnehmen
make up	erfinden	*take to*	(auf Anhieb) mögen
pick out	aussuchen	*wait for*	warten auf
pick up	aufheben, sich aneignen	*wake up*	aufwachen, wecken
		wash up	spülen, abwaschen

'It's difficult at first. But you'll soon pick it up.'

N I'll **wash** **up** ***the glasses.***
I'll **wash** ***the glasses*** **up.**

But only:
I'll **wash** ***them*** **up.**

The word order in sentences made up of phrasal verbs with an adverbial particle (*off, out, up, away,* etc.) and an object, is as follows:
If the object is a noun, the particle can be placed either before the object or after it.
But if the object is a personal pronoun, the particle always comes after it.

7 Verbs with two objects

1. *Give* and other verbs in this category

	Subject	Verb		Direct object (usually a thing)	
1.	Mr Miller	gave	the waiter	a ten-pound note.	
2.	Mr Miller	gave		a ten-pound note	to the waiter.

Indirect object (usually a person)

Give and other verbs in the same category (see list below) take two objects: a direct object (usually referring to a thing) and an indirect object (usually referring to a person).
Sentences containing these objects can be formed in two different ways:

- The indirect object is used **without a preposition** and comes **before** the direct object (example 1).
- The indirect object is used **with the preposition *to*** and comes **after** the direct object (example 2).

Common verbs used in the same way as *give*:

bring (herbringen)
take (hinbringen)
hand (reichen)
lend
offer
pass (reichen)
promise (versprechen)
sell
send
tell
show
write

'Take this cake to Grandmother.'

'Oh, you've brought me a cake. How nice!'

Position of the two objects: this depends on their length and their importance to the sentence

The shop assistant showed | Sarah (**Indirect object**) | lots of pretty blouses. (**Direct object**)

She sold | fifty postcards (**Direct object**) | to a group of American tourists from Texas. (**Indirect object**)

The longer of the two objects generally comes at the end of the sentence.

They've sent | my brother (**Indirect object**) | a record (**Direct object (stressed)**) | (and not the cassette that he asked for).

While we were away, the postman handed | all our letters, newspapers and parcels (**Direct object**) | to the neighbours. (**Indirect object (stressed)**)

If one of the objects is emphasized more strongly than the other (e.g. to show a contrast), it comes at the end.

N 1 What have you done with that magazine I lent you? – I've given **it *to* my sister.**
Can I see your photos of Wales? – Of course. I'll show **them *to* you** now.

If the direct object is a pronoun that refers to a thing or things (*it* or *them*), the indirect object (with *to*) usually comes after it.

N 2 She bought **her cat** some fish, and she got some bones ***for* the dog.**
Sie kaufte ihrer Katze etwas Fisch und sie holte ein paar Knochen für den Hund.

In the case of *get (holen), buy, make* and *order*, the indirect object can be put either before or after the direct object. If it comes after the direct object, *for* is used instead of *to*.

2. *Explain* and other verbs in this category

Subject	Verb	Direct object (usually a thing)	Indirect object (usually a person)
The teacher	explained	the meaning of the poem	**to** the pupils.

First direct object, then indirect object (always with *to*)

Dr Fairweather **described the effects of the medicine *to* my mother.**
... beschrieb meiner Mutter die Wirkungen des Medikaments.
Did he say anything about the new pills? – No, he didn't **mention them *to* me.**
Nein, er hat sie mir gegenüber nicht erwähnt.
May I **suggest something *to* you**?
Could you please **dictate that sentence *to* us** again?

The indirect object of *explain, describe* and other verbs in the same category is always introduced by *to*. It usually appears after the direct object.

Common verbs used in this way:

announce	ankündigen	*describe*	beschreiben	*introduce*	vorstellen	*say*	sagen
deliver	liefern	*dictate*	diktieren	*mention*	erwähnen	*suggest*	vorschlagen

⚠ He didn't { **tell *us*** anything / **say** anything ***to us*** } about his plans.

In sentences with *tell*, the indirect object follows the verb without *to*.
In sentences with *say*, however, the indirect object is always introduced by *to*.

N 1 The headmaster explained ***to* the parents** the main advantages of the new examination system.

The headmaster explained	***to* the parents**	the main advantages of the new examination system.
	Indir. object	**Direct object**

It is also possible for the indirect object to come before the direct object. This word order is sometimes used if the direct object is very long, or is especially stressed.
Notice that *to* is **always** used before the indirect object, whichever word order is chosen.

N 2 See § 80 for verbs with two objects in passive sentences.

§ 98 Verbs with object + object complement

Subject	Verb	Object	Object complement
The settlers	called	**America**	**the New World.**
Many of them	found	**life**	**hard.**

After certain verbs, an object complement is used after the object. This complement can be either a noun or an adjective.

Use of the object complement: with and without a preposition

The gold in California attracted thousands of pioneers, but it didn't **make** them all **rich**.
Today many people still **regard** America **as the land of endless opportunities.**
The Americans **chose** George Washington **as their leader** during the War of Independence.
Later they **elected** him **President**, and after his death they **called** their new capital city **Washington** after him.

After some verbs, a preposition is used between the object and the object complement; after other verbs, no preposition is used.

Without a preposition:	With a preposition (*as* or *for*):
make *(someone happy)*	***regard*** *(s.th.)* ***as*** *(certain)*
find *(something interesting)*	***recognize*** *(s.th.)* ***as*** *(a fact)*
call *(s.o. a snob)*	***think of*** *(s.th.)* ***as*** *(natural)*
think *(s.o. intelligent)*	***look upon*** *(s.o.)* ***as*** *(a hero)*
appoint *(s.o. captain)*	***choose*** *(s.o.)* ***as*** *(one's leader)*
elect *(s.o. president)*	***take*** *(s.o.)* ***for*** *(a fool)*

N Most settlers **considered** it **(as) their right** to take land belonging to the Indians.

Consider can be used with or without *as* before the complement.

9 Verbal expressions for German adverbs

In German, personal attitudes are often expressed with the help of adverbs; in English, however, verbal expressions are more common. (Compare *etwas* ***gern*** *tun* in German with ***like*** *doing s.th.* in English.) Some of these verbal expressions are followed by an *-ing*-form or an infinitive; others are followed by a *that*-clause. The following table includes the most common examples of verbal expressions in English that correspond to constructions with adverbs in German:

Likes and dislikes: *be fond of/like/hate/... + -ing*-Form	
Kate **is fond of** sing**ing** Irish folk songs. She **likes** play**ing** the guitar, too.	Kate singt **gern** irische Volkslieder. Sie spielt auch **gern** Gitarre.
I **hate** writ**ing** letters, I **prefer** ring**ing** my friends up.	Ich schreibe **sehr ungern** Briefe, ich rufe meine Freunde **lieber** an.
Patrick **loves** walk**ing** in the mountains. He **enjoys** climb**ing**, too.	Patrick macht **sehr gern** Bergwanderungen. Er klettert auch **gern**.
Regrets, hopes, expectations: *I'm afraid/I hope/I suppose/ ... + that*-clause	
I'm afraid (that) I can't come with you on Saturday.	Ich kann am Samstag **leider** nicht mitkommen.
I hope you have a great time.	**Hoffentlich** habt ihr viel Spaß.
I expect/suppose we'll be back quite late.	Wir kommen **vermutlich** ziemlich spät zurück.

Certainty, probability, chance: ***be sure to/be likely to/seem to/happen to/...*** **+ infinitive**	
We**'re sure to** win the match next weekend. I think we**'re certain to** get into the next round.	Wir werden das Spiel ... **sicher** gewinnen. Ich glaube, wir kommen **bestimmt** ...
The weather **is likely to** stay fine. Summer **seems to** have come at last.	Das Wetter bleibt **wahrscheinlich** schön. Der Sommer ist **anscheinend** endlich gekommen.
There are a lot of cars outside the Browns'. They **appear to** have visitors.	... Sie haben **anscheinend** Besuch.
I **happened to** meet some old friends of mine at Dave's birthday party.	Ich traf **zufällig** ein paar alte Freunde ...

See § 81 for passive constructions with the infinitive such as *be said to, be supposed to* corresponding to German *angeblich, vermutlich.*

Continuation of an activity or habit: ***go on/keep (on)*** **+ *-ing*-form**	
I told the boys to come to the table, but they just **went on** play**ing** football.	..., aber sie spielten einfach **weiter** Fußball.
No wonder you're always tired. You **keep** go**ing** to bed so late.	... Du gehst **dauernd** so spät ins Bett.

See § 92 for the construction *used to* + infinitive corresponding to German *früher* or *immer.*

'We seem to have lost our way!'

Chapter 12: The infinitive

100 Forms and functions of the infinitive

1. Forms

The infinitive, like the gerund and the participle, is one of the non-finite forms of the verb (see also § 112 and § 121). The non-finite verb forms, unlike the finite forms, give no indication of grammatical person and number:

Carol	**travels**	a lot.	Finite verb form (3rd person singular)
Carol wants	**to travel**	all over the USA.	Infinitive

The infinitive can be formed with all verbs except the modal auxiliaries (*can, must,* etc.). It can appear with or without *to*.

Alan *wants* **to join** the orchestra.	The infinitive with *to* is used after a large number of main verbs.
Peter *can* **play** the piano. His parents *made* him **learn** the violin. Why don't they *let* Sally **take** singing lessons?	The infinitive without *to* is used – after most modal auxiliaries (see also § 86) – after a few other verbs, e.g. *make* and *let* (see also § 105)
I'd rather **play** the guitar than the piano. *We'd better* **practise** this piece again together before the concert.	– after expressions such as *I would rather (ich würde lieber), I had better (ich sollte lieber).*
Your old cello could **be repaired,** couldn't it? Concerts like this ought **to be advertised** better.	The passive infinitive is formed with *(to) be* and the past participle.

1 Less common forms:

I've just heard from the Jacksons. They seem **to be having** a great time in Colorado.	the progressive form of the infinitive: *(to) be* + present participle
The Whites' luggage has gone. They appear **to have left** already. The beds ought **to have been made** before the guests arrived.	the perfect forms of the infinitive: – active: *(to) have* + past participle – passive: *(to) have been* + past participle

2 We decided **not to go** to the concert after all. — Wir entschlossen uns, doch nicht ... zu gehen.

If only the infinitive is negated, and not the whole sentence, *not* comes before the infinitive.

2. Functions in the sentence

Infinitive constructions can have several different functions in the sentence.
They are especially common in the function which nouns normally have. They can appear

Subject

To sail across the Atlantic The voyage across the Atlantic	was an enormous adventure in the days of Columbus.	– (rarely) as the subject of a sentence

Object

Sailors in those days did not expect	**to travel in comfort.** a comfortable journey.	– as the object

Infinitive constructions can also appear

	Adverbial		
The old sailing ships took weeks	**to get to America.** for the voyage to America.		– as an adverbial
	Attribute		
The best time	**to start** for the journey	was the early summer.	– as an attribute to a noun (here: *time*)

3. The use of the passive forms of the infinitive

He decided **to call** the police.
(Compare: He **called** the police.)
They asked **to be informed** at once.
(Compare: They **were informed** at once.)

Large cities usually have a high crime rate. But that is, of course, **to be expected.**
Aber das ist natürlich **zu erwarten.**
It remains **to be seen** whether traffic on this road will be less heavy when the new motorway is finished. Es bleibt **abzuwarten,** ob ...

The infinitive usually appears in the active form.

The passive form is used only if the verb in a corresponding simple sentence is also in the passive.

After *be* and *remain*, the passive infinitive is used when the meaning is passive.
In German, however, the active form of the infinitive is used here, although the meaning is passive.

§ 101 The 'object + infinitive' construction

		Infinitive	
Dad wants		**to cut the hedge.**	Papa möchte (selbst) die Hecke schneiden.
	Mark	**to cut the hedge.**	Papa möchte, daß Mark die Hecke schneidet.
	Object +	**infinitive**	

Verbs such as *want* can be followed directly by an infinitive (see also § 103). But it is also possible to put an object (here a noun: *Mark*) between the verb and the infinitive. This object can be seen as the 'notional' (or 'logical') subject of the infinitive construction.

Dad wants ***me*** **to cut the hedge.**	Papa möchte, daß ich die Hecke schneide.

If a personal pronoun is used here instead of a noun, it is used in the object form (here: *me*). For this reason, it is usual to call the construction the 'object + infinitive' construction.

102 The infinitive construction with *for*

		Infinitive	
It is important		**to send those letters off today.**	Es ist wichtig, diese Briefe heute abzusenden.
It is important	***for those letters***	**to arrive tomorrow.**	Es ist wichtig, daß diese Briefe morgen ankommen.
	***for* + object +**	**infinitive**	

Hasn't the postman come yet? It's unusual ***for him*** **to be late.** — Es ist ungewöhnlich, daß er zu spät kommt.

It's normal ***for letters and cards*** **to take longer at Christmas time.** — Es ist normal, daß Briefe in der Weihnachtszeit länger brauchen.

After expressions such as *it is important, it is unusual, it is normal, it is a pity,* a noun or pronoun (in the object case) can come before the infinitive, but it must be introduced by *for.* This construction with *for* usually corresponds to a *daß*-clause in German.

N The infinitive construction with *for* is also used

– to express a purpose or a result (especially in sentences with *too* and *enough*),

Here are some sandwiches ***for you* to eat on the journey.**
Hier sind ein paar belegte Brote, die du auf der Reise essen kannst.
This coffee is **too hot *for me* to drink.**
Dieser Kaffee ist zu heiß, als daß ich ihn trinken könnte.
Judy wants to watch 'The Third Man', but I'm afraid we won't be back **early enough *for her* to see it.**
... wir kommen nicht so rechtzeitig zurück, daß sie ihn sehen kann.

– after certain verbs that take *for,* e.g. *wait for, arrange for.*

We'd better not leave the house yet. I'm still **waiting *for Jane* to ring up.**
... Ich warte immer noch darauf, daß Jane anruft.
I've **arranged *for a taxi* to pick you up at nine.**
Ich habe vereinbart/es so eingerichtet, daß ein Taxi euch um neun abholt.

103 The infinitive after verbs expressing a wish or expectation

***want, wish, like, expect* (+ object) + infinitive**	
The construction without an object	**The construction with an object**
We **want to go** up into the mountains this weekend. Wir wollen dieses Wochenende in die Berge fahren. We **expect to leave** early on Monday morning. Steve **would like to fly** to Canada next summer. Please apply immediately if you **wish to take part** in the course.	We **wanted *Chris* to come** with us, but he can't. Wir wollten, daß Chris mitkommt, ... We **expect *the coach* to leave** at six thirty. **Would** you **like *me* to take** you to the airport? There will be a special meeting for parents who **wish *their children* to take part** in the French exchange.

Want, wish, would/should like and *expect* can be followed either by the infinitive alone, or by an 'object + infinitive' construction. (See also § 101.)

N **I'm planning to do** a lot of work these holidays.
Do you still **intend to read** that book I lent you?
I **hope to** finish 'War and Peace' this weekend.

The verbs *plan, intend, hope* can be followed only by an infinitive **without** an object. *Hope* is often followed by a *that*-clause: *I hope (that) you do well in your exam.*

§ 104 The infinitive after verbs expressing commands or requests, advice or warnings

tell, ask, advise, warn **+ object + infinitive**	
Isn't Dave here yet? I **told *him* to wait** for us outside the cinema.	Ich habe ihm gesagt, er solle vor dem Kino auf uns warten.
I **advise *you* to leave** the car here and go by Underground.	Ich rate euch, den Wagen hierzulassen ...
Where's Julia? Dad **asked *her* to be** back by eleven.	Papa hat sie gebeten, bis elf zurück zu sein.
I **warned *the children* to stand** well back when the train came in.	Ich ermahnte die Kinder, Abstand zu halten, ...
The ticket collector **warned *them* not to open** the door while the train was still moving.	Der Schaffner warnte sie davor, die Tür zu öffnen, ...
This construction is used to express commands in reported speech (see also § 152).	

⚠ to warn s.o. **to do** s.th. — jdn. ermahnen, etwas zu tun
to warn s.o. **not to do** s.th. — jdn. davor warnen, etwas zu tun

'I warned you not to leave the window open.'

§ 105 The infinitive after verbs of causing or allowing

German *lassen* + infinitive can have two meanings: to **cause** something, or to **allow** something. These different meanings are expressed by different verbs in English.

Causing: ***make/have*** **+ object + infinitive without *to***	**Allowing:** ***let*** **+ object + infinitive without *to***
Mrs Baker **made *the boys* fasten** their seat belts before she drove off. Mrs Baker ließ die Jungen sich anschnallen, ... Speed limits are the only way to **make *people* drive** more slowly. ... das einzige Mittel, die Leute dazu zu bewegen, langsamer zu fahren. I'll **have *you* pay** for the damage you caused. Ich lasse Sie den Schaden ... bezahlen!	Sally easily gets car-sick. We'd better **let *her* sit** at the front. Wir lassen sie besser vorne sitzen. I'll collect you in Mum's car, if she **lets *me* have** it tonight. Ich hole dich in Muttis Wagen ab, wenn sie mir erlaubt, ihn heute abend zu nehmen.
Make is used in the sense of 'cause or force someone to do something'/'cause something to happen'. *Have* can also be used in this sense, but *make* is usually preferred. (See § 124 for *have* + object + past participle.)	*Let* is used in the sense of 'allow someone to do something'/'allow something to happen'.

1 You can't **force *people* to use** public transport.
An accident on the motorway **caused *traffic* to come** to a standstill.
I expect Dad will **allow *me* to take** his racing-bike.

After *force* and *cause* (used instead of *make*) and after *allow* (used instead of *let*), the infinitive **with** *to* is used.

2 I **was made to open** both my bags when we went through the customs.

Make sometimes appears in the passive. In this case, it is followed by the infinitive **with** *to*.

06 The infinitive after verbs of perception and observation

see, hear, feel, notice, watch, observe **+ object + infinitive without *to***

I **heard** the doorbell **ring**. It must be the Browns.	Ich habe es klingeln hören.
Did you **see** them **come** to the front door?	Hast du sie zur Haustür kommen sehen?
Mrs Jones **noticed** two boys **come** into the shop.	Mrs Jones bemerkte, daß zwei Jungen in den Laden kamen.
She **saw** them **take** a packet of sweets and **run** off.	Sie sah, wie sie eine Packung Bonbons nahmen und wegliefen.

The German equivalent of this construction can be either an infinitive construction (like in English) or a subordinate clause introduced by *daß* or *wie*. (See § 123 for participles used after verbs of perception and observation.)

N A young man in jeans and a black leather jacket **was seen to enter** the building at exactly 9.45.

If these verbs (i.e. of perception and observation) are used in the passive, the infinitive takes *to*.

'Could you tell me where to park the car?'

07 The infinitive after interrogatives

	Interrogative + infinitive		
Could you tell me	**where**	**to park**	the car?
	where	I can park	the car?
	Indirect question		

I don't know **what to do** this afternoon.	... what I should do this afternoon.
We had no idea **which** way **to go**.	... which way we had to go.
They had to ask a policeman **how to get** back to the main road.	... how they could get back ...
He wondered **whether to walk** to the village or **to go** by car.	... whether he should walk ...

Instead of using a subordinate clause containing an interrogative (or *whether*) and *should/can/could/must/have to,* it is more common to use a shorter construction consisting of interrogative + infinitive. In German, however, a subordinate clause has to be used (e.g. *Ich weiß nicht, was ich heute nachmittag tun soll).*

§ 108 Infinitives instead of relative clauses with modal auxiliaries

He gave me a list of books	**Infinitive construction**	Er gab mir eine Liste von Büchern, die ich für das neue Schuljahr kaufen soll.
	to buy for the new school year.	
	which I should buy for the new school year.	
	Relative clause	

I offered Aunt Alice some magazines **to read.** (... which she could read.)
'Frankenstein' isn't exactly the film **to watch before you go to bed.** (... which you should watch ...)
There's a special button **to press** (... which you can press) if you want the video text.

The infinitive in this construction expresses a duty or a possibility.

N Ireland is an ideal place **to spend a quiet holiday.** (... a place where you can spend ...)
The time **to go to the Lake District** is the spring or early summer. (... the time when you should go ...)

Infinitive constructions after expressions of place or time correspond to subordinate clauses with *where* or *when* and a modal auxiliary.

§ 109 The infinitive after *the first, the last, the only one*

The Soviet Union was **the first nation**	**Infinitive construction**	The infinitive can be used after numerical expressions like *the first, the last* and *the only.* This construction corresponds to a relative clause.
	to send a man into space.	
	that sent a man into space.	
	Relative clause	

Neil Armstrong was **the first (man) to set foot on the moon.**
Of all the continents, Australia was **the last to be discovered.**
Amundsen and his team weren't **the only men to reach the South Pole in 1911.**
But they were **the only ones to return.**

The first and *the last* can be used with or without a noun. *The only,* however, must be followed by a noun or by the prop word *one/ones.*

N In 1976, a 12-year-old boy from Kent became **the youngest person to swim the English Channel.**

This infinitive construction can also be used after superlatives.

10 The infinitive to express a purpose

	Infinitive construction
We walked right to the edge of the cliffs	**(in order) to get the best view of the coastline.**
	so that we would get the best view of the coastline.
	Adverbial clause of purpose

The infinitive here is used to express a purpose. For emphasis, *in order to* can be used instead of *to*. This infinitive construction corresponds to an adverbial clause of purpose (see also § 129.2.). The infinitive construction is generally preferred, as it is shorter and less clumsy.

Trick photography is often used **to create the special effects in films.**
Die Trickfotografie wird oft benutzt, um die besonderen Effekte in Filmen zu erzeugen.
This camera is designed **to be used with a telephoto lens.**
Diese Kamera ist so konstruiert, daß sie mit einem Teleobjektiv benutzt werden kann.

N The built-in flash is used ***for taking* photographs in poor light or indoors.**

Be used can also be followed by *for* + gerund.

Uncle George stepped back in order to get the best view.

11 The infinitive to express a comment

To be honest, I didn't think much of the play last night.	Ehrlich gesagt, ...
To tell you the truth, I didn't enjoy it at all.	Um die Wahrheit zu sagen, ...
To put it plainly, the actors were completely hopeless.	Schlicht und einfach gesagt, ...

These infinitive constructions correspond to adverbs of comment such as *frankly, surely, honestly,* etc. They are normally used at the beginning of a sentence, and are usually separated from the rest of the sentence by a comma.

We didn't have a very good weekend in London.	
To start with, it rained all the time from the moment we arrived.	Es fing damit an, daß ...
We went the wrong way on the Underground twice at least, and I lost my London Explorer ticket.	
To cut a long story short, the whole trip was a disaster.	Kurz und gut, ...

These infinitive constructions are used as an introduction (e.g. *to start with, to begin with*), or as a way of summarizing (*to sum up, to cut a long story short*). They correspond to linking adverbials such as *firstly, all in all,* etc. (see also § 145).

N See § 99 for the infinitive after verbs and verbal expressions referring to certainty, probability and chance (*be sure, seem, happen,* etc.).

Chapter 13: The gerund

§ 112 Forms and functions of the gerund

1. Forms

Like the infinitive and the participle, the gerund is one of the non-finite forms of the verb (see also § 100 and § 121).

I really like **living** in New York.	The gerund, just like the present participle, is formed with the infinitive of the verb + *-ing;* for this reason, it is also called the *-ing*-form.
At first, my sister and I were a little afraid of **being sent** to an American school.	The passive form of the gerund is made up of *being* and the past participle.

N 1 The gerund can also appear in the perfect form (active and passive), although this is less common.

I think I remember **having seen** that girl at the athletics meeting last June.	Active: *having* + past participle
My brother is so proud of **having been chosen** for the school football team.	Passive: *having been* + past participle

N 2 I enjoy lying in the sun and ***not*** **doing** anything.

The negative is formed by placing the word *not* directly before the gerund construction.

2. Functions in the sentence

The gerund is the form of the verb that is nearest in function to a noun. The fact that gerunds can be used after prepositions makes this similarity clear (e. g. *She is fond of* ***horses*** *– she is fond of* ***riding***).

	The gerund can appear
Subject **Travelling all day** / Long journeys can be very tiring.	– as the subject of a sentence
Object I'm looking forward to **seeing you**. / your visit.	– as the object of a sentence
Adverbial You can't get on the plane **without showing your ticket.** / without a ticket.	– as an adverbial
Attribute Is there no chance **of going to Paris again next year?** / of another trip to Paris next year?	– as an attribute to a noun.

N Jenny's latest hobby *is* **rock-climbing.**
My main interest *has* always *been* **cross-country skiing.**

The gerund is also used as a subject complement (after the verb *be*).

13 The gerund with a subject of its own

Aunt Sarah doesn't like watching horror films.

Aunt Sarah doesn't like Steve watching horror films.

Aunt Sarah **doesn't like**		**watching**	horror films.	Tante Sarah sieht nicht gerne Gruselfilme an.
Aunt Sarah **doesn't like**	***Steve***	**watching**	horror films.	Tante Sarah hat es nicht gern, daß **Steve** Gruselfilme ansieht.
	Notional subject	**gerund**		

The gerund can appear directly after verbs such as *like, hate, don't mind.*
It is also possible, however, to place a noun (here: *Steve*) between the verb and the gerund. In this way, the gerund is given a subject of its own (also called the 'notional' – or 'logical' – subject).
This construction usually corresponds to a *daß*-clause in German.

I hope you **don't mind** { ***me* opening** the window. / ***my* opening** the window. }
Ich hoffe, es macht Ihnen nichts aus, wenn ich das Fenster öffne.

If the notional subject is a pronoun, it usually appears in the object case (*me, him, them,* etc.); it can also appear as a possessive determiner (*my, his, their,* etc.), although this is less common.

Next week at this time Alan will be here. **I'm** really **looking forward to *him* coming.**
... Ich freue mich wirklich darauf, daß er kommt.
Tell your friends **I've nothing against *them* talking** to you on the phone,
but **I'm tired of *them* ringing** up late at night.
..., ich habe nichts dagegen, wenn sie..., aber ich habe es satt, daß sie...

The gerund with a notional subject of its own can also appear after expressions with prepositions.

N Have you heard about { ***Susan* getting** a place at Oxford? / ***Susan's* getting** a place at Oxford? }

If the notional subject of the gerund construction is a noun referring to a person, it can appear as an *s*-genitive form, although this is unusual.

§ 114 The gerund after verbs without a preposition

***like, enjoy, start, stop, (don't) mind, suggest,* etc. + gerund**

I **like walking** in the woods in all weathers.
Everyone **enjoys sitting** by the fire when it's cold outside.

My brother lives nearer the office now, so he has **started cycling** to work.
We've **stopped playing** tennis in the evenings now. It's simply too dark.

I **don't mind looking** after Tommy if you want to go out.
Mike **suggests getting** a babysitter for Saturday evening.

Further examples of common verbs that can be followed by the gerund:

love, prefer, hate, dislike, *can't stand* (nicht ausstehen können) — *begin, finish* — *avoid* (vermeiden) — *practise*

Some of these verbs can also be followed by the infinitive (see § 115).

§ 115 Gerund and infinitive after certain verbs

Same meaning	
It **started snowing** last night. If it **continues being** so cold, we'll be able to skate on the lake soon. I **like skiing,** but not when it's as cold as this!	It **started to rain** when we got off the bus. The weather improved steadily and temperatures **continued to rise.** We **like to have** our meals outside in hot weather.

In the case of the verbs *start, begin, continue, like, love, prefer* and *hate,* there is practically no difference in meaning between the gerund and the infinitive construction.

⚠ **Would you like to hear** my new cassette? – **I'd like to record** that song.

Only the infinitive can be used, however, after *would/should like* and the short forms *I'd like, we'd like,* etc.

N My bike **needs *cleaning* / needs *to be cleaned.*** Mein Fahrrad muß geputzt werden.

After the verb *need,* the gerund is passive in meaning. It is also possible to use the passive form of the infinitive here, instead of the gerund.

Different meaning	
Gerund after *stop:* refers to the activity so far	**Infinitive after *stop:* refers to a new activity**
Please **stop talking** about food all the time – you know how hungry I am!	This Chinese restaurant looks good. Let's **stop to look** at the menu for a moment. (= Let's stop walking in order to look ...)
The gerund refers to the activity that comes (or has come) to an end.	The infinitive expresses the intention to do something else.

Gerund after *remember, forget, regret:* refers to what has already happened (backward in time)	**Infinitive after *remember, forget, regret:* expresses an intention (forward in time)**
Surely you've got Kevin's address! I **remember writing** it down for you only a few days ago. John was only three when we left Glasgow. He has completely **forgotten living** there. Fiona quickly **regretted moving** into that flat on the main road. She hadn't realized how noisy it was.	Please **remember to post** that letter when you go out this afternoon. Oh dear! I **forgot to give** Lucy that book when she left. Now I'll have to send it by post. At least I **remembered to get** her address. We **regret to tell** you that all our rooms are already booked for the whole of July and August.
The gerund refers to an action or event that has already taken place (examples 1 and 2), or that took place before a certain time in the past (example 3).	The infinitive refers to what is still to be done at present (examples 1 and 3), or to what was still to be done in the past (example 2).

1 I **mean to find out** whether Jane Brown still lives in Birmingham.
Ich beabsichtige herauszufinden, ob ...
That **means looking** through all the Browns in the telephone book!
Das bedeutet (hat zur Folge), daß ich alle Browns im Telefonbuch durchgehen muß.

The infinitive after *mean* is used to express an intention.
The gerund after *mean* is used to express a consequence or result.

2 The little girl **tried to open** the door, but she couldn't quite reach the handle.
Das kleine Mädchen versuchte, die Tür zu öffnen, ...
I can't open this parcel, the string's been tied too tightly. – Why don't you **try cutting** it with a pair of scissors?
... – Warum versuchst du es nicht mit einer Schere? (Warum versuchst du nicht, das Paket zu öffnen, indem du die Schnur mit einer Schere durchschneidest?)

The infinitive after *try* expresses an attempt.
The gerund after *try* expresses a new method of doing something or 'trying something out'.

Not many succeed in reaching the top.

6 The gerund after verb + preposition

***succeed in, dream of, look forward to,* etc. + gerund**	
Lots of people go into show business, but not many **succeed in reaching** the top.	..., aber es gelingt nicht vielen, an die Spitze zu kommen.
Have you ever **thought of going** to drama school?	Hast du je daran gedacht, zur Schauspielschule zu gehen?
I've always **dreamed of playing** in a rock group.	Ich habe immer davon geträumt, ... zu spielen.
The Dubliners are giving a concert here next month. We're all **looking forward to going.**	... Wir freuen uns alle darauf, hinzugehen.

Further examples of common verbs followed by a preposition + gerund:

complain about	sich über etwas beschweren	*insist on*	auf etwas bestehen
worry about	sich wegen etwas Sorgen machen	*rely on*	sich auf etwas verlassen
talk of/about	von etwas reden		

⚠ He was **looking forward to** { his holiday. / **going** on holiday. }

Notice that the word *to* in the expression *look forward to* is a preposition; it is **not** part of the infinitive. For this reason, it is always followed by a gerund (or a noun).

He's fond of reading detective stories.

§ 117 The gerund after adjective + preposition

***be fond of, be (no) good at, be interested in,* etc. + gerund**

I'm fond of reading detective stories,	Ich lese gern Kriminalgeschichten,
but **I'm no good at guessing** 'who did it'!	aber ich kann nicht gut raten, wer der Täter war.
Are you **interested in looking** around that second-hand bookshop with me?	Hast du Interesse daran, dich mit mir in dieser Antiquariatsbuchhandlung umzuschauen?

These combinations of *be* + adjective often correspond to English or German verbs (e. g. ***be fond** of s.th.* = ***like** s.th; **be interested** in s.th.* = ***sich** für etwas **interessieren***). For this reason, they are called 'verbal expressions' (see also § 99).

Further examples of common verbal expressions followed by preposition + gerund:

be proud of	stolz auf etwas sein	*be keen on*	auf etwas aus sein, etwas gern tun
be ashamed of	sich für etwas schämen	*be good/bad at*	etwas gut/schlecht können
be afraid of	Angst vor etwas haben	*be famous for*	bekannt/berühmt für etwas sein
be tired of	einer Sache müde/überdrüssig sein	*be crazy about*	verrückt nach etwas sein

N My parents **are used to hearing** our music. — Meine Eltern sind es gewohnt, unsere Musik zu hören.
My parents **used to listen** to pop music when they were young. — Meine Eltern hörten sich immer Popmusik an, ...

In the verbal expression *be used to (es gewohnt sein)*, the word *to* is a preposition (as in *look forward to,* see § 116) and is followed by a gerund. The *to* in *used to (pflegte, tat etwas früher)*, however, is part of the infinitive (see § 92).

§ 118 The gerund after noun + preposition

***(be in) danger of, (have) difficulty in, (the) idea of,* etc. + gerund**

We**'re in danger of running** out of petrol.	Wir laufen Gefahr, daß uns das Benzin ausgeht.
We **had difficulty in getting** spare parts for the car when it broke down in Spain.	Wir hatten Schwierigkeiten, Ersatzteile für den Wagen zu bekommen, ...
The **idea of driving** all the way down to Greece in that old van is quite absurd.	Die Idee, in diesem alten Lieferwagen bis ganz nach Griechenland hinunterzufahren, ...

Further examples of nouns followed by preposition + gerund:
(a) chance of, (an) opportunity of, (a) way of, (the) possibility of.

N When Columbus discovered America, he was really looking for a new **way of reaching / to reach** India.
After he had returned to Spain, he soon had another **chance of exploring / to explore** the new continent.

After *chance, way* and *opportunity,* it is also possible to use the infinitive with *to.*

.9 Preposition + gerund as an adverbial

The gerund after *on, for, in spite of*

Preposition + gerund:	***On arriving*** **at his hotel,**	Mr O'Leary sent a telegram to his wife.
Subordinate clause:	As soon as he arrived at his hotel,	
	Sobald er in seinem Hotel ankam,	...
Preposition + gerund:	***In spite of setting*** **off early,**	we missed the ferry we had booked.
Subordinate clause:	Although we set off early,	
	Obwohl wir früh losfuhren,	verpaßten wir die Fähre ...

The taxi driver expected a good tip	***for managing*** **to get us to the airport in time.**	Preposition + gerund
	because he had managed to get us ...	Subordinate clause

Der Taxifahrer erwartete ein anständiges Trinkgeld dafür, daß / weil er es geschafft hatte, ...

Gerund constructions of this kind correspond to subordinate clauses.

N Make sure you've filled in the form correctly **before sending** it off.
Vergewissere dich, daß du das Formular richtig ausgefüllt hast, bevor du es abschickst.
After looking at all the brochures, we finally decided to book a week in Vienna.
Nachdem wir alle Broschüren angeschaut hatten, ...

Constructions with *before/after* + *-ing*-form also correspond to subordinate clauses. The *-ing*-form can be seen either as a gerund (*before/after* as a preposition, followed by the gerund), or as a participle (*before/after* as a conjunction, followed by the present participle). (See also § 126.2.)

The gerund after *instead of, by, without, apart from, as well as*

Peter has decided to look for a job **instead of staying** on at school.	... anstatt auf der Schule zu bleiben.
He earned some money last summer **by working** for the Post Office.	..., indem er bei der Post arbeitete.
She made a bad impression at the interview. She just came in **without knocking.**	... Sie kam einfach herein, ohne anzuklopfen.
Apart from being a qualified nurse, Caroline is also an experienced cook.	Abgesehen davon, daß sie eine ausgebildete Krankenschwester ist, ...
She works part time **as well as doing** all the housework.	... Sie arbeitet halbtags und macht noch zusätzlich die ganze Hausarbeit.

There are no subordinate clauses in English that correspond to gerund constructions with *instead of, by, without* and *apart from.* In German, these constructions can correspond to infinitive constructions, subordinate clauses, or main clauses.

'How about going by taxi?'

§ 120 The gerund after expressions like *it's no use, there is no, what about*

It's no use ringing the bell – they're obviously out.	Es hat keinen Zweck zu klingeln ...
It's no good calling for Dad – he's gone to the office.	Es nützt nichts, nach Papa zu rufen ...
There's no knowing what may happen if you leave that dog alone in the house.	Man kann nie wissen, was passiert, ...
What about/How about inviting the Watsons to supper tomorrow?	Wie wär's, wenn wir Watsons morgen zum Abendessen einladen würden?
It's worth going down to Carter's for the vegetables – they're quite a bit cheaper there.	Es lohnt sich, zu Carter zu gehen, um Gemüse zu kaufen ...

⚠ **It's no use *complaining*** about the price of food. ***But:*** **It's not very useful *to write*** a shopping list and then leave it at home.

It's no good *asking* for strawberries in January. ***But:*** **It's not good *to keep*** food in the fridge too long – it may go bad.

Notice that the construction *'it is* + adjective' is normally followed by the infinitive (see § 102). There are only very few expressions with *it is* that are followed by the gerund.

Chapter 14: Participles

21 Forms and functions of participles

1. Forms

The participle, like the infinitive and the gerund, is one of the non-finite forms of the verb, since it gives no indication of grammatical person or number (see also § 100 and § 112).
There are two types of participles:

Examples	Explanation
We watched the workmen **pulling** down the house. I talked to one of the men **working** on the building-site. We watched the house **being pulled** down. **Having shown** us his plans, the architect then told us about prices. The old town hall is now a very attractive building, **having been** completely **modernized.**	1. The present participle This is formed with the infinitive of the verb and the ending *-ing*. For this reason, it is also called the *-ing*-form. (See § 57 for the spelling of the present participle.) Other forms of the present participle: – the simple passive form (*being* + past participle) – the perfect form in the active (*having* + past participle) in the passive (*having been* + past participle).
I noticed some young trees **planted** at the side of the road. The village church, **built** in Norman times, is famous for its beautiful windows.	2. The past participle Regular forms consist of the infinitive of the verb and the ending *-ed*. (See § 58 and § 60 for the spelling and pronunciation of the past participle.) The past participles of irregular verbs are listed in Appendix 1 on pages I-III.

2. Functions in the sentence

	Attribute		**Complement**
The captain of the	**damaged** **sinking** old	ship remained	**unmoved.** **standing on deck.** silent.

Both the present participle and the past participle are often used in the same way as an adjective – either as an attribute to a noun, or as a complement after certain verbs.

Adverbial

When leaving the harbour, When we left the harbour,	we saw the Isle of Wight against the sunrise.
When informed of the emergency, When they were informed ...,	the passengers rushed to the lifeboats.

Both types of participle can be used in adverbials (here: of time). These adverbials correspond to subordinate clauses.

As can be seen from the examples, the present participle is active in meaning, and the past participle is passive in meaning.

We stood watching the sunset ...

§ 122 Participles after verbs describing a position or movement

Verbs such as *sit, stand, lie, remain, come, go* + present participle

He never goes out. He just **sits watching** TV.
Er **sitzt** nur da **und sieht** fern.
They **stood waiting** outside the cinema for twenty minutes. Sie **standen** ... **und warteten.**
We can't **stay talking** here all day. Wir können nicht den ganzen Tag hier**bleiben und reden**.
They **remained sitting** at the table long after the meal was over. Sie **blieben** ... **sitzen** ...
When I was at the bus stop yesterday, a small boy **came running** up to me. ..., **kam** ein kleiner Junge auf mich zu**gelaufen**.

The present participle after these verbs is used to show that another action is going on at the same time.
To express the same meaning in German, two verbs joined by the word *und* are generally used.

After certain verbs, however, the German equivalent of the English present participle is either an infinitive or a past participle.

Verbs such as *remain, lie* + past participle

The drinks were popular, but most of the food **remained untouched**. ... **blieb unberührt**.
It was unusually cold. Even the beach **lay covered** in snow. ... **lag** schnee**bedeckt** da.

The past participle after these verbs expresses the result of an action taking place before (here: nobody had touched the food; snow had covered the beach).
The German equivalent is also a past participle.

§ 123 Participles after verbs of perception and observation

***see, hear, feel, notice, find, watch, observe* + object + present participle**

Some of the neighbours **watched** us **moving** in.
Einige Nachbarn schauten zu, wie wir einzogen.
I **heard** Susan **talking** on the telephone.
Ich hörte Susan telefonieren.
I **didn't see** her **leaving** the house.
Ich sah nicht, wie sie das Haus verließ.

This construction corresponds to an infinitive construction in German, or to a subordinate clause introduced by *wie*.

Some of the neighbours watched us moving in.

N Mr Macdonald **was** last **seen leaving** the Black Lion at 9.45 last night.

This construction can also be used with the passive forms of *see, hear, watch* and *find*.

Comparing the use of participle and infinitive after verbs of perception and observation	
Present participle: **emphasis on the activity in progress**	**Infinitive:** **emphasis on the action as a whole**
Do you **hear** those people **speaking** German? I think they must be Austrians. We **noticed** Mr Smith **planting** a new hedge when we went past.	I **heard** the doorbell **ring** once, but when I looked, there was nobody there. We **saw** the man **open** the car door, **put** in the box and **drive** off.
The present participle is used to describe an activity in progress, especially when only a part of the activity is observed (and **not** the whole activity from beginning to end). Here, the use of the present participle corresponds to that of the progressive form (i. e. Mr Smith **was planting** a new hedge when we went past).	The infinitive is used when an action is observed from beginning to end. This is especially the case when a short action or a series of actions is described. Here, the use of the infinitive corresponds to that of the simple form (i. e. The man **opened** the door, **put** in the box and **drove** off). (See § 106 for the use of the infinitive.)

4 Participles after *have* and *get* meaning 'to cause'

have/get + object + past participle	
We always **have** the car **washed**. We never have time to do it ourselves.	Wir **lassen** den Wagen immer **waschen.**
Your jacket looks good. – Yes, I **had** it **cleaned** last week.	..., ich **habe** sie ... **reinigen lassen**.
My watch doesn't work properly any more. – Well, why don't you **get** it **repaired**?	... – Warum **läßt** du sie nicht **reparieren**?

Have can be used in this construction in both formal and informal style. *Get,* however, is only used in colloquial (informal) English.

		Object		
She usually	**has**	her hair	**cut**	at the hairdresser's.

Sie **läßt** sich die Haare gewöhnlich beim Friseur **schneiden**.

		Object	
She	**has cut**	her hair	herself this time.

Sie **hat** sich diesmal die Haare selbst **geschnitten**.

It is important not to confuse the construction *have* + object + past participle with the present perfect (or past perfect). The position of the object shows which construction is which.

Comparing the use of non-finite constructions after verbs of causing and allowing		
My grandparents **have** their grass **cut** by a gardener. The garage door looks shabby. We must **get** it **repainted.**	Dad always **makes** me **mow** the lawn. He hates doing it himself. Yesterday he even **had** me **cut** the hedge.	Please **let** me **plant** the apple tree. I'm sure I can do it on my own. Uncle Fred never **lets** the children **climb** the trees in his garden. He thinks it's too dangerous.
To **cause** something to be done: *have* } + object + past *get* } participle	To **cause** or **force** someone to do something: *make* } + object + infinitive *have* } without *to* (see § 105)	To **allow** someone to do something: *let* + object + infinitive without *to* (see § 105)

N I **left** Susan at the coach station. — Ich verließ Susan am Busbahnhof.
Don't **leave** the camera in the car. — Laß den Fotoapparat nicht im Auto liegen.
Who**'s left** the window open? — Wer hat das Fenster offengelassen?

The verb *leave*, **not** *let*, is used when the meaning is *verlassen/zurücklassen/ an einem bestimmten Ort lassen/in einem bestimmten Zustand lassen* in German.

§ 125 Participles used instead of relative clauses

	Participle construction/ Relative clause				
The black girl			***waiting***	**at the bus stop**	is one of my sister's friends.
	who	***is***	***waiting***	**at the bus stop**	
Many of the people			***living***	**in this area**	are Asians.
	who		***live***	**in this area**	
Most of the things			***sold***	**in this shop**	come from India.
	which	***are***	***sold***	**in this shop**	

↑ **Subject of the relative clause**

These participle constructions correspond to relative clauses in which the relative pronoun is the subject. The present participle is used when the verb in a corresponding relative clause would be in the active voice; the past participle is used when the verb would be in the passive voice.

126 Participle constructions used as adverbials

1. Participle constructions without conjunctions

Participle constructions corresponding to subordinate clauses

Present participle Subordinate clause	**Looking down from the plane,** When we looked down from the plane, Als wir ... herunterschauten, ...	we saw the lights of the city below.
Present participle (negative form) Subordinate clause	**Not knowing much about the climate in Australia,** As they didn't know much about ..., Da sie nicht viel ... wußten, ...	the visitors were surprised by the very hot weather.
Present participle (perfect form) Subordinate clause	**Having travelled so far the first week,** As they had travelled so far ..., Da sie ... so weit gereist waren, ...	they were glad to have a rest for a few days.
Past participle Subordinate clause	**Warned about the dangers of the strong sunlight,** As I had been warned about ..., Da ich ... gewarnt worden war, ...	I decided to buy a sunhat.

These participle constructions can be seen as shortened adverbial clauses.
Constructions with the present participle correspond to clauses containing active verbs; those with the past participle correspond to clauses containing passive verbs.
The negative is formed by placing *not* (or *never*) before the participle.
As can be seen from the examples, participle constructions of this kind mostly correspond to adverbial clauses of time (example 1) or of reason (examples 2–4). (See § 129 for adverbial clauses.)

Having a warm climate and beautiful golden beaches, Australia is ideal for bathing and surfing. Most of the population live in towns and cities along the coast, so

This kind of participle construction generally sounds very formal, and is used mainly in written English.

The tourists followed the guide up the hill, **taking photos and admiring the view.**
Die Touristen folgten dem Reiseleiter ... Sie machten Fotos und bewunderten die Aussicht.

The construction with the present participle is also often used to describe accompanying circumstances; in this case, it usually comes at the end of the sentence. In German, a second main clause is generally used as an equivalent of the participle construction.

2. Participle constructions with conjunctions

***While* staying in Detroit,** I met one of my old Cambridge friends.
While I was staying in Detroit, ...

***Though* trained as a chemist,** he was now working in the auto industry.
Though he was/had been trained as a chemist, ...

His wife had prepared a very large meal, **as if expecting more than one visitor.**
..., as if she was expecting more than one visitor.

Like subordinate clauses, participle constructions can be introduced by conjunctions (e. g. *while, though, as if*). The meaning of the participle construction depends on which conjunction is used. (See § 129 for the use of conjunctions.)

§ 127 Participle constructions with subjects of their own

Absolute participle constructions used instead of subordinate or main clauses

		Notional subject		Subject	
Participle		**The weather**	***being* foggy,**	our plane	was not able to land.
Sub. clause	As	the weather	was foggy,		
Participle		**The runways**	***cleared* of snow,**	passengers were at last allowed to go on board.	
Sub. clause	When	the runways	had been cleared ...,		

Subject		Notional subject		
The stewardess	led the way to the plane,	**the tourists**	***following* with their hand luggage.**	Participle
The stewardess	led the way to the plane.	The tourists	followed with their hand luggage.	Second main clause

These participle constructions do not depend on the subject of the main clause (here: *our plane, passengers, the stewardess*), but have a subject of their own (also called the 'notional' – or 'logical' – subject of the participle construction; here: *the weather, the runways, the tourists.*)
Participle constructions of this kind are also called 'absolute participle constructions'.
They correspond to adverbial clauses of reason or time, or – especially when they appear at the end of the sentence – to a second main clause.

The '*with* + participle' construction

It's been a very busy day, ***with* the telephone *ringing* all the time.**	Es war ein sehr arbeitsreicher Tag. Das Telefon klingelte pausenlos.
I can't work properly ***with* all that noise *going* on.**	Ich kann nicht richtig arbeiten, wenn so ein Lärm herrscht.
***With* so many people in the office *being* ill just now,** there's twice as much to do as usual.	Da so viele Leute im Büro jetzt krank sind, ...
***With* autumn *coming on* and the days *getting* shorter,** Ben has given up jogging after work.	Jetzt wo der Herbst kommt und die Tage kürzer werden, ...

⚠ Absolute participle constructions are often introduced by *with.*
The word *with* has no equivalent in German, and cannot be translated by German *mit.* Instead, it is usual to start a new sentence, or to use a subordinate clause introduced by *als, während, wenn, da, wobei* or *indem,* depending on the context.
Absolute participle constructions sound very formal when they are not introduced by *with.* The *with* construction, however, is very common, and is used in everyday spoken English as well as in the written language.

Chapter 15: Subordinate clauses

28 Types of subordinate clauses

Complex sentence		
Adverbial clause	**Main clause**	**Relative clause**
Before I went on holiday,	I made a list of the things	that I wanted to pack.

The complex sentence is made up of a main clause together with one or more subordinate clauses. Subordinate clauses are usually connected to the main clause by conjunctions (e.g. *before, because*), by relative pronouns (e.g. *who, which, that*) or by interrogatives (e.g. *why, what*).

The film **(that/which) I saw with Peter last week** was fantastic.
I didn't realize **(that) you had seen it before.**

I wonder **where Dad put the Radio Times.**

I'll switch off **as soon as the programme is over.**

There are several different types of subordinate clauses:

- relative clauses (see §§ 130–137)
- *that*-clauses (see § 150: reported or indirect statements)
- reported or indirect questions (see § 152)
- adverbial clauses (see § 129).

29 Adverbial clauses

1. Function and position

Adverbial clause	▶ **When we had had lunch,**	we sat in the garden for an hour.
Adverbial phrase	▶ *After our meal*	

I'll ring you up	**before I leave.**	◀ Adverbial clause
	tomorrow morning.	◀ Adverbial phrase

Adverbial clauses have the same function as adverbial phrases (in the examples above, they are adverbial clauses and phrases of time). These clauses are introduced by a conjunction such as *when, before* or *because.*
If an adverbial clause appears at the beginning of the sentence, a comma usually separates it from the main clause. But if the sentence starts with the main clause, there is generally no comma.

When	I	saw	her,	I	recognized	her	at once.
Als	ich	sie	sah,	erkannte	ich	sie	sofort.

Unlike in German, the word order in the subordinate clause and in the main clause is always: subject – verb – object.

'She takes her dog with her wherever she goes.'

2. Types of adverbial clauses and conjunctions

Adverbial clauses can be divided into different groups, according to their meaning. For each group, there are a number of typical conjunctions.

Adverbial clauses of time: *while* (während), *after* (nachdem), *since* (seit) etc.

Grandma often falls asleep ***while* she's watching TV.**	..., während ...
***After* our friends had left,** we switched on the late night news.	Nachdem ...
Have you read any books ***since* the holidays started?**	..., seit ...

Further conjunctions belonging to this group:

as soon as	sobald	*till/until*	bis	*when*	als, wenn
before	bevor	*(not ...) until*	(erst ...), wenn	*whenever*	immer wenn, wann auch immer

Adverbial clauses of place and direction:
***where* (wo, wohin), *wherever* (wo/wohin auch immer)**

Some of the scenes in 'West Country Magic' were filmed ***where* we used to live.**	... dort ..., wo ...
John takes his camera with him ***wherever* he goes.**	..., wohin er auch geht.

Adverbial clauses of reason: *because* (weil), *as/since* (da)

My parents listen to the radio a lot ***because* they're both keen on music.**	..., weil ...
***As* we couldn't get tickets for the concert,** we decided to go to the cinema.	Da ..., ...
***Since* there's nothing good on TV tonight,** let's have a game of cards.	Da ..., ...

Subordinate clauses introduced by *because* usually come after the main clause, but those introduced by *as* and *since* often appear at the beginning of the sentence.

Adverbial clauses of concession and contrast:
***although/though/even though* (obwohl), *whereas* (während, wohingegen)**

***Although* my sister works at the library,** she doesn't read many books herself.	Obwohl ...
We still take two Sunday papers, ***even though* we never find time to read them properly.**	..., obwohl ...
A paper provides all the news in detail, ***whereas* TV only gives you the main points.**	..., während/wohingegen ...

Adverbial clauses of condition:
if **(wenn, falls),** ***even if*** **(selbst wenn),** ***unless*** **(sofern nicht, außer wenn, es sei denn)**

You'll spoil your eyes ***if*** **you read in this bad light.**	..., wenn ...
I'm going to finish 'War and Peace', ***even if*** **it takes me ages to get through.**	..., selbst wenn ...
I'll throw this magazine away, ***unless*** **you want to keep it.**	..., es sei denn ...

The simple present (never the *will*-future) is used in most subordinate clauses introduced by *unless*, while the *will*-future is used in the main clause.
See § 73 for the use of tenses in conditional sentences with *if*.

Adverbial clauses of comparison: ***as if /as though*** **(als ob)**

The dog sat in front of the TV screen ***as if*** **it was watching the programme.**	..., als ob er die Sendung anschauen würde.
I said good morning, but John went on reading the paper ***as though*** **he hadn't heard.**	..., als hätte er nichts gehört.

Adverbial clauses of purpose and result:
so that **(damit),** ***so/such ... that*** **(so/solch ..., daß)**

Let's leave for the show in good time ***so that*** **we get good seats.**	..., damit ...
I've got ***so*** many records ***that*** **I don't know where to put them all.**	... so viele Schallplatten, daß ...
The fans made ***such*** a noise ***that*** **we couldn't hear the music properly.**	... einen solchen Lärm, daß...

I haven't heard from Linda ***since*** **she wrote last Christmas.**	..., seit sie ...
We'll have to write them a letter, ***since*** **we don't know their telephone number.**	..., da wir ...

Since has two different meanings: It can introduce
– an adverbial clause of time (*seit* in German)
– an adverbial clause of reason (*da* in German).

0 Defining and non-defining relative clauses

Defining relative clauses	Non-defining relative clauses
Captain Cook was the man **who first explored the coasts of Australia.**	Captain Cook, **who was born in Yorkshire,** was one of the most famous English explorers.
Many of the animals **which live in Australia** are unknown in other parts of the world.	The kangaroo, **which is found only in Australia,** can jump as high as ten feet in the air.
A defining relative clause gives a **definition** of its antecedent (here: *the man, the animals*). It explains who or what is meant (i.e. *which man? which animals?*), and is therefore necessary to the sense of the whole sentence. No commas are used to separate a defining relative clause from the rest of the sentence. Similarly, no pause is made in speaking.	A non-defining relative clause contains extra (but basically unnecessary) information. If it were left out, the rest of the sentence would still make perfect sense. Commas are used to separate a non-defining relative clause from the rest of the sentence. In speaking, pauses are made.

⚠ Colloquial English:

My father was born in India. He's never liked the English climate.

Formal style:

My father, who was born in India, has never liked the English climate.

Non-defining relative clauses usually appear only in formal style. In colloquial English, they are generally avoided, and two separate sentences are used instead.

§ 131 The relative pronouns *who, which* and *that* in defining relative clauses

Who/that **for persons**	***Which/that*** **for things**
The man *who/that* owns this restaurant comes from Hong Kong. Do you know the girls ***who/that* have just come in?**	Is this the table ***which/that* was reserved for us?** These must be the stairs ***which/that* go down to the Saxon Bar.**

Who refers only to persons, *which* only to things.
That can refer to both persons and things.
Who, which and *that* are used for both singular and plural.

Who, which **and *that* as the subject and as the object of relative clauses**

	Subject
Is that the waiter	***who/that* served us yesterday?**
Ist das der Kellner,	**der** uns gestern bediente?
	Object
Look, that's the boy	***who/that* we saw in the café.**
Schau mal, das ist der Junge,	**den** wir im Café gesehen haben.
	Subject
I don't like cheese	***which/that* tastes too strong.**
Ich mag keinen Käse,	**der** zu streng schmeckt.
	Object
The waitress brought me a hamburger	***which/that* I hadn't ordered.**
Die Kellnerin brachte mir einen Hamburger,	**den** ich nicht bestellt hatte.

Who, that and *which* remain unchanged, whether they are used as the subject or as the object of a relative clause.

*'That's the dog that she takes for walks.' – 'You mean: that takes **her.**'*

1 The President was a man ***whom* many will remember as a friend.**

Whom can be used as the object as well as *who*.
Whom sounds very formal, however, and is used chiefly in written English.

2 I've marked **all** the TV programmes ***that* I want to see this week.**
We don't watch **anything *that* goes on after midnight.**
'High Noon' is one of the **best** Westerns ***that* I've ever seen.**

That is more commonly used for things than *which*. *That* is especially preferred after *all, something, anything, everything, nothing, the first, the last*, and after superlatives.

32 Contact clauses

	Defining relative clause	
	Object	
Here's a photo of the American girl	***that/who***	**we met on the coach tour.**
	—	**we met on the coach tour.**
Is that the camera	***that/which***	**you bought in London last year?**
	—	**you bought in London last year?**

When the relative pronoun is the object of the relative clause, it is very often left out.
(It can also be left out in relative clauses with verb + preposition: see § 133.)
Relative clauses without a relative pronoun are called 'contact clauses'; this is because they are in direct 'contact' with the antecedent (here: *the American girl, the camera*).
Contact clauses are preferred especially in colloquial English, and when the relative clause is short (e.g. *I like the jacket you're wearing*).

	Subject	
Did you notice the boy	***who***	**came in just now?**
I think that was the boy	**we**	**met at the Longs'.**

The relative pronoun cannot be left out if it is the **subject** of the relative clause. The relative clause **must** have a subject, whether this is a relative pronoun or – as in contact clauses – another pronoun or noun.

33 Prepositions in defining relative clauses

This is the family	—	**I stayed**	***with***	**in Exeter.**	Dies ist die Familie, bei der ich in Exeter wohnte.
	that	**I stayed**	***with***	**in Exeter.**	
	who	**I stayed**	***with***	**in Exeter.**	
	with whom	**I stayed**		**in Exeter.**	
I still remember the house	—	**I lived**	***in***	**as a child.**	Ich erinnere mich noch an das Haus, in dem ich als Kind wohnte.
	that	**I lived**	***in***	**as a child.**	
	which	**I lived**	***in***	**as a child.**	
	in which	**I lived**		**as a child.**	

In a defining relative clause, the preposition usually comes after the verb.
In this case, the relative pronoun is often left out, i.e. a contact clause is used (see also § 132).
In contact clauses, as well as in relative clauses with *that* and *who*, the preposition **always** comes after the verb.
In formal style, the preposition can appear before the relative pronoun. In this case, *whom* or *which* are used (never *who* or *that*).

N 1 The McKees? Who are they? – They're the people **we got that card *from*.**
Alison McKee and I were at school together. She was the girl **I shared a room *with*.**

If the verb in the relative clause has a direct object, the preposition comes after this object.

N 2 We visited the house **where** (in which) Shakespeare was born.
The guide told us a few details about the time **when** (at which) he lived.

If the antecedent refers to a place or time, the relative clause can be introduced by *where* or *when*.

§ 134 Relative pronouns in non-defining relative clauses

My Uncle Edward, ***who* was a taxi driver in London,** emigrated to Australia as a young man.
He has three grown-up sons, ***whom* I have never met.**
The Huntleys, ***with whom* I stayed last summer,** have a house on the coast. Huntleys, bei denen ich letzten Sommer wohnte, haben ein Haus an der Küste.

The Opera House, ***which* is the most famous building in Sydney,** was built in the 1970s.
Mary showed us some photos of the Grand Canyon, ***which* she had visited on her tour.**
We walked up the cliff path, ***from which* there was a wonderful view of the bay.** Wir gingen den Pfad zu den Klippen hoch, von dem aus man eine wundervolle Aussicht auf die Bucht hatte.

Non-defining relative clauses **always** contain a relative pronoun.
- For persons, *who* is used when the relative pronoun is the subject, and *whom* is used when it is the object or when a preposition is used.
- For things, *which* is used.

The preposition usually comes before the relative pronoun, as it does in German.

⚠ *That* can never be used in non-defining relative clauses.

'That's the boy I told you about, you know, the one whose parents are vegetarians.'

§ 135 Relative clauses with *whose*

I was talking to a girl ***whose uncle* lives in Darwin.**	..., dessen Onkel...
Are those the people ***whose car* broke down in the Outback?**	..., deren Wagen...
Australia, ***whose 200th 'birthday'* was celebrated in 1988,** is the only nation that is also a continent.	..., dessen 200. ‚Geburtstag' ...

It is also possible to introduce relative clauses with the relative determiner *whose* + noun.
Whose expresses a relationship which would normally be expressed by the genitive or a possessive determiner (e.g. *the girl's/her uncle*).
Whose can refer to both persons and things. It can be used in defining and in non-defining relative clauses.

1 The thieves stole the car from a garage, **the door of which** had been left open. ..., deren Tor ...

In formal style, *of which* is sometimes used instead of *whose* when referring to things.

2 Fighting broke out among the supporters, **a number of whom** were arrested. ..., von denen eine Anzahl ...
The fans started throwing bottles, **one of which** injured a player. ..., von denen eine ...

After expressions of quantity such as *a number, one, both, many* and *most, of whom* is used when referring to persons and *of which* when referring to things.

6 *Which* referring to a whole sentence

Our hotel was a long way from the centre of the town, ***which* was a disadvantage, of course.**
..., was natürlich ein Nachteil war.
We took a taxi to the airport, ***which* saved us a bit of time.**
..., was uns etwas Zeit sparte.

As well as referring to a single noun, *which* can be used to refer to a whole sentence.
Which corresponds in this case to German *was*. The function of the relative clause is to give a comment on the whole of the sentence it refers to.
Relative clauses of this type are always non-defining, and are therefore separated from the main clause by a comma.

7 Relative clauses with *whoever, whatever, whichever*

I don't mind how many people come round on Saturday.
You can invite ***whoever* you like.** — Du kannst einladen, wen (auch immer) du willst.
***Whatever* happens,** you can depend on me. — Was auch passiert, ... / Egal was passiert, ...
It'll be a great match, ***whichever* team wins.** — ..., ganz gleich welche Mannschaft gewinnt.

The addition of *-ever* turns *who, what* and *which* into 'generalizing relative pronouns' meaning 'it doesn't matter who/what/which' (in German: *wer/was/welcher auch immer; jeder, der; alles, was*).
A relative clause containing a generalizing relative pronoun has no antecedent in the main clause.

Chapter 16: Affirmative and negative statements, questions, shortened sentences

§ 138 Affirmative and negative statements

Word order in affirmative statements

	Subject	Verb	Rest of the sentence
	My brother	speaks	five languages.
	I	have translated	that Italian letter now.

The usual word order in affirmative statements is: 1. subject – 2. verb – 3. rest of the sentence. This rule also applies to compound tenses (e. g. *have translated*).

Last autumn	we	went	to Paris for a week.
When I go to San Francisco,	I	will send	you a card of the Golden Gate Bridge.

The basic word order subject – verb – rest of the sentence remains unchanged even when the sentence begins with an adverbial phrase or a subordinate clause.
Compare English and German:

Last autumn	we	went	to Paris.
Letzten Herbst	fuhren	wir	nach Paris.

Word order in negative statements

Subject	Auxiliary + *n't*	Main verb	Rest of the sentence
I	**can't**	**understand**	this poem.
I	**haven't**	**read**	anything by Shakespeare before.
We	**don't**	**know**	the play at all.
John	**doesn't**	**like**	going to the theatre.
He	**didn't**	**come**	with us to 'Romeo and Juliet'.

Negative statements are formed by adding *n't* to the auxiliary. If there is no auxiliary in the corresponding affirmative sentence (e. g. *We know ..., John likes ...*, etc.), a negative form of *do (don't/doesn't/didn't)* is used instead. (The verb *be* is an exception. See § 83.2.)

In formal style the long form of the auxiliary + *not* is used:
Prices are for bed and breakfast only. They ***do not include*** *an evening meal.*

N 1 We **don't have** eggs for breakfast every morning.

The verb *have* forms its negative with *do,* but only when it is used as a main verb (see also § 84.2).

N 2 We sat down at one of the tables, but **nobody** came to serve us.
No wonder you're hungry. You had **nothing** for lunch.
We **never** watch TV while we're having a meal.
Could you go down to the shops? There's **no** milk left.

Negative statements can be formed with other words apart from *not;* the most common are *nobody, nothing, never* and *no.*

9 Imperative sentences

Affirmative imperatives
Come in. Komm (Kommt/Kommen Sie) herein!
Sit down, please.
Have a cup of tea.
Be careful, you two.
Watch out! There's a car coming.
Stop barking, Rover. Hör auf zu bellen, Rover!

The imperative form of the verb is the same as the infinitive form, both in the singular and in the plural.
Like in German, the imperative is used to express requests, invitations, warnings or orders.

A full stop is generally used after imperatives in English. An exclamation mark is only used in the case of very strict orders or warnings, or when the person speaking is very angry or excited. (See example 5: *Watch out!)*

Negative imperatives
Don't be silly.
Don't forget to post my letters.
Please **do not walk** on the grass.
Never swim in cold water after a meal.

Negative imperatives are formed with *don't* (or *do not* in formal style) + infinitive.

They can also be formed with *never* + infinitive.

Imperatives with *let's*
Let's have our picnic here.
Machen wir unser Picknick hier.
Oh no, **let's not stop** now, **let's go** on a bit further.
Nein, halten wir lieber jetzt noch nicht, fahren wir noch ein bißchen weiter.

Imperatives in which the speaker includes him- or herself are formed with *let's/let's not* + infinitive. The long form *let us* is used only in very formal style (e. g. *Let us pray – Lasset uns beten).*

0 *Yes/no* questions

Yes/no questions are questions which expect either *yes* or *no* as an answer. They are never introduced by an interrogative (e. g. *when, where, who*).

The auxiliary in *yes/no* questions

Auxiliary	Subject	Main verb	Rest of the sentence
Is	it	**raining?**	
Shall	we	**go**	for a walk?
Would	you	**like**	to come with me?
Do	you	**understand**	this sentence?
Does	Janet	**speak**	French?
Did	I	**pronounce**	your name wrong?

'Can't you read?'

Yes/no questions are always introduced by an auxiliary.

If there is no auxiliary in the corresponding affirmative statement (e. g. *I understand this sentence*), the question must be introduced by *do, does* or *did.*

Negative *yes/no* questions			
Auxiliary + *n't*	**Subject**	**Main verb**	**Rest of the sentence**
Can't	you	**open**	that bottle?
Doesn't	Ben	**like**	orange juice?
Didn't	the milkman	**come**	this morning?
Does this government **not spend** enough on space projects already?			

Negative *yes/no* questions are formed by adding *n't* to the auxiliary at the beginning of the sentence.

In formal style, the long form *not* comes after the subject.

§ 141 Questions with interrogatives

Questions of this type begin with an interrogative (also called a question word). The interrogative can stand alone (*Who ...? Why ...?*, etc.), or it can be followed by a noun or an *of*-phrase (*What countries ...? Which of them ...?*, etc.).

When the interrogative is the subject		
Interrogative	**Verb**	**Rest of the sentence**
Who	**discovered**	Australia?
What countries	**belong to**	the Commonwealth?
Which of them	**will take part**	in the Commonwealth Games next year?

Questions in which the interrogative is the subject (or part of the subject) take the same word order as affirmative statements (see § 138). The auxiliary *do* is **not** used in these questions.

When the interrogative is not the subject				
Interrog.	**Auxiliary**	**Subject**	**Main verb**	**Rest of the sent.**
Where	**shall**	we	**go**	tonight?
When	**are**	we	**leaving**	on Saturday?
What	**have**	you	**packed**	for the weekend?
How long	**do**	you	**want**	to stay in town?
Why	**doesn't**	Dave	**post**	your letters?
Who	**did**	you	**talk to**	on the phone?

When the interrogative is **not** the subject (or part of the subject), the word order is the same as in *yes/no* questions (see § 140).

If there is no auxiliary in the corresponding affirmative statement, the auxiliary *do* has to be used.

'Which of you did the cooking?'

Notice the difference in use between *what, who* and *which:*

What are you going to have?
Was nimmst du?
What vegetables have you got?
Was für Gemüse haben Sie?
Who made this delicious cake?
Wer hat diesen leckeren Kuchen gebacken?

What is used to ask about things and *who* to ask about persons when there is a possible choice from an **unlimited number.**

Which would you prefer – tea or coffee?
Was hättest du lieber – Tee oder Kaffee?
Which of these apples are best for cooking?
Welche von diesen Äpfeln eignen sich am besten zum Kochen?
Which of you broke this plate?
Wer von euch hat diesen Teller zerbrochen?

Which is used to ask about things or persons when the choice of possibilities is **limited to a certain number.** *Which* is often followed by an *of*-phrase. (*What* or *who* can never be used before an *of*-phrase!)

2 Question tags

Question tags are used in English when expecting someone to agree with what one says, or to confirm it. They are added at the end of a statement. In German, expressions such as *nicht wahr? oder?* or *oder nicht?* are used in this sense.

Affirmative statement: Negative question tag					**Negative statement: Affirmative question tag**				
Dad	**is**	**working,**		**isn't** he?	He	**isn't**	**using**	the phone,	**is** he?
Gill	**will**	**be**	here soon,	**won't** she?	You	**won't**	**be**	late,	**will** you?
You	**have**	**got**	time now,	**haven't** you?	You	**haven't**	**got**	a key,	**have** you?
The Smiths		**live**	here,	**don't** they?	Ian	**doesn't**	**go**	to your school,	**does** he?
You		**met**	Sarah once,	**didn't** you?	You	**didn't**	**meet**	her sister,	**did** you?

The question tag repeats the contents of the sentence in shortened form, as auxiliary and subject.
The subject always appears as a personal pronoun.
If there is no auxiliary in the sentence, a form of *do* is used in the question tag.
An affirmative statement is followed by a negative question tag.
A negative statement is followed by an affirmative question tag.

1 **There's** a post box round the corner, **isn't there?**

If *there* is the 'formal subject' of the sentence, it appears again in the question tag (see also § 143 N and § 146).

2 **Let's have** a cup of tea, **shall we?**
Get the milk out of the fridge, **will you?**
Help yourself to biscuits, **won't you?**

Imperatives beginning with *let's* take the question tag *shall we?*
After other imperatives, *will you?* is used; *won't you?* is sometimes used in polite offers.

3 We **must** leave now, **mustn't** we?

After *I must/we must* etc., the question tag is *mustn't I?/mustn't we?* etc.
(However, the negative short answer to the question *Must I?/Must we?* is always *No, you needn't.* See also § 90, page 86 ⚠.)

Intonation (the rising and falling of the voice) in question tags	
Our train leaves at 9.47, **doesn't it?** ↗ – Yes, it does. We don't have to change at Bristol, **do we?** ↗ – No, I don't think so.	It's a lovely day, **isn't it?** ↘ The countryside looks beautiful at this time of year, **doesn't it?** ↘
Rising intonation is used for the question tag in situations where the speaker is not sure whether the statement is correct or not. An answer to the question is expected.	Falling intonation is used for the question tag when the speaker has no doubts about the statement, and naturally supposes that the other person will agree. An answer to the question is not necessarily expected.

'It's a lovely day, isn't it?'

§ 143 Short answers

In English, the answers to *yes/no* questions are very often phrased as short answers, unlike in German, where the answer *ja* or *nein* usually stands alone.

Auxiliary	Subject	Main verb	Rest of the sentence		Subject	Auxiliary
Have	you	got	a good map of London?	– Yes, – No,	I I	**have.** **haven't.**
Can	you	remember	the name of that bookshop?	– Yes, – No,	I I	**can.** **can't.**
Will	the museum	be	open tomorrow?	– Yes, – No,	it it	**will.** **won't.**
Do	the Jacksons	live	in Wimbledon?	– Yes, – No,	they they	**do.** **don't.**
Does	Mr Jackson	work	in the City?	– Yes, – No,	he he	**does.** **doesn't.**
Did	you	miss	your train yesterday?	– Yes, – No,	I I	**did.** **didn't.**

The auxiliary used in the question appears again in the short answer. The subject appears as a personal pronoun.

N **Is there** a telephone box near here? – Yes, **there is.** / No, **there isn't.**

If *there* is the 'formal subject' of the question, it appears again in the short answer (see also § 142 N 1 and § 146).

144 Short sentences with *so, nor, neither*

Short sentences with *so, nor* and *neither* are used as a way of commenting on a statement that has just been made. They correspond to short sentences with *auch, auch nicht* in German.

So **after affirmative statements**

Subject	Auxiliary	Main verb	Rest of the sentence		Auxiliary	Subject	
I	**am**	**feeling**	hungry!	– So	**am**	I.	Ich auch.
I	**can**	**smell**	the eggs and bacon.	– So	**can**	I.	Ich auch.
Peter		**likes**	cornflakes for breakfast, and so		**does**	Jane.	... Jane auch.

The auxiliary used in the first sentence appears again in the short sentence. If there is no auxiliary in the first sentence, *do, does* or *did* must be used. The subject of the short sentence comes at the end; this gives it extra emphasis.

Neither/Nor **after negative statements**

Subject	Auxiliary (negative)	Main verb	Rest of the sentence		Auxiliary	Subject	
I	**have never**	**tried**	Mexican food before.	– Neither – Nor	**have** **have**	I. I.	Ich auch nicht.
We	**don't**	**like**	that new pizza place in Queen Street.	– Neither	**do**	we.	Wir auch nicht.
Sue and Paul	**aren't**	**going**	to the barbecue tonight.	– Nor	**are**	Tracey and Mike.	

N Paul doesn't like curry. – **I don't either** (instead of: **Neither do I.**)
I'm terribly thirsty. – **I am, too.** (instead of: **So am I.**)

Short sentences made up of subject + negative auxiliary + *either* are often used in colloquial English instead of the construction with *neither/nor.*
Too can be used in a similar way instead of the construction with *so.*
(See § 145.2 for more about the use of *either* and *too.*)

Chapter 17: From sentence to text (linking and emphasis)

§ 145 Conjunctions and adverbs used to link sentences or parts of a sentence

1. Conjunctions, adverbs, and combinations such as *either ... or*

The streets in this part of York are very narrow, **and** most of the houses are very old. We can take the bus to the town centre, **or** we can walk there, of course. There's a car park near the Minster, **but** it's usually full at this time of day. In the summer months, York is full of visitors, **for** it is of great historical interest.	Whole sentences or parts of a sentence can be linked together with the conjunctions *and, or, but (aber, sondern)* and *for (denn).*
For centuries York was one of the most important cities in the North; **yet** it was never spoilt by industry. We've lived in the city centre for ten years now, **so** we're used to the noise of traffic. Millions of pounds have been spent on repairing the Minster; **however,** a lot of work still has to be done.	Linking adverbs such as *yet (doch, dennoch, trotzdem), so (deshalb, daher), however (jedoch)* can be used in the same way.
We could **either** look round the museum, **or** we could go on one of those river trips. What bad luck! **Neither** the castle **nor** the gardens are open to the public on Sundays. The Black Lion is the best hotel here. It has **both** an outdoor **and** an indoor swimming-pool.	The following combinations can also be used for linking: *either...or (entweder...oder), neither...nor (weder...noch), both...and (sowohl...als auch).*

N Further examples of adverbs used for linking:

therefore	deshalb, daher	*nevertheless*	trotzdem, dennoch,
after all	schließlich, immerhin	*anyway*	jedenfalls, sowieso, trotzdem
on the one hand ...	einerseits ...	*though*	aber, doch
... on the other hand	... andererseits		

Though in this sense comes at the end of the sentence, and is usually separated from the rest of the sentence by a comma:
We had a lovely walk along the beach; it was too cold to go swimming, though. ..., aber es war zu kalt zum Schwimmen.

'Well, what do you think? We can either swim, or we can try the bridge.'

2. English equivalents of the German adverb *auch*

The adverbs *too, as well, also, (not ...) either* are also used for linking.

When we were in York, we visited the Minster, of course, and we went to the Castle Museum, **too.** ...und wir gingen **auch** ...
Did you go to the Railway Museum **as well?** Seid ihr **auch** ... gegangen?
No, we didn't. And we did**n't** have time for a trip down the river **either.** ... Und wir hatten **auch keine** Zeit für ...

But we enjoyed walking through the streets, and we **also** did a bit of shopping.
... und wir haben **auch** ein bißchen eingekauft.

In affirmative statements, *too, as well* and *also* are used.

In negative statements (after *not, never,* etc.), *either* is used.
Too, as well and *either* come at the end of the sentence.
Also, however, normally takes mid position (before the main verb, or between the auxiliary and the main verb).

I like eggs.	– I like them, **too.**	Ich esse sie **auch** gern.
We don't often have fish for lunch.	– We **don't either.**	Wir **auch nicht.**

Unlike German *auch, too* can only be used in affirmative sentences. In negative statements, *either* must be used.

6 The *there* construction

There is/There are **+ notional subject**

Formal subject	*be*	Notional subject	Rest of the sentence	
There	**is**	a big new shoe shop	in the High Street.	In der Hauptstraße gibt es/ist ...
There	**were**	a lot of people	at church this morning.	Heute morgen waren viele Leute ...

Sentences with *be* are often introduced by *there* (which is always unstressed). This 'formal subject' is followed by a form of *be,* and then by the actual subject of the sentence, the 'notional subject'.

Formal subject	*be*	Notional subject	Participle	Rest of the sentence	
There	**are**	several taxis	**waiting**	outside the station.	Vor dem Bahnhof warten ...
There	**was**	a big American car	**parked**	in front of the house.	Gestern abend parkte ...

A present or past participle can also be included in the *there* construction. Sentences of this kind generally correspond to a normal affirmative sentence in German.

The use of the *there* construction in context

There was an accident in the High Street on Saturday morning. A lorry braked suddenly at the traffic lights and a car ran into the back of it. Luckily nobody was injured, but the front of the car was badly damaged and the police had to be called.
There was a short report about it in the local paper on Monday. As usual, the reporter had got some of the details wrong.

The *there* construction is often used as a way of introducing a new theme or topic, e. g. to start a new phase of a text or a conversation.

§ 147 The *it is/it was* construction

It is/It was as a way of emphasizing part of a sentence

	Subject	Verb	Object	Adverbial
Simple sentence:	Captain Cook	discovered	Hawaii	in 1779.

It was Captain Cook who discovered Hawaii (and not Columbus).
It was Hawaii that Captain Cook discovered (not Australia).
It was in 1779 that he discovered Hawaii (not in 1789).

It is/It was can be used to emphasize practically any part of a sentence (except the verb). The rest of the sentence follows in the form of a relative clause or a *that*-clause.

⚠ **It *was* the natives** in Hawaii that killed Captain Cook.

The singular form *it is/it was* is used even when the noun that follows is in the plural.

The use of the *it is/it was* construction in context

At the beginning of the 19th century, most people in Britain still lived in small villages. Many of them never left the area in which they were born. News travelled slowly from place to place, and the horse was still the fastest form of transport. **It was the development of the railways** that changed all this.

Excuse me. Is this the train to Reading? – No, it goes straight through to Paddington, sir. **It's the next one** that stops at Reading.

The *it is/it was* construction is generally used as a way of expressing a contrast or of correcting a mistake or misunderstanding.

'The design's all right.
It's the price I'm not so keen on.'

§ 148 Emphatic use of *do*

Apart from their function in questions and negative statements, *do, does* and *did* can be used as a way of giving affirmative statements extra emphasis.

Stressing a contrast

We *don't* buy much food at the health food shop. But we **do** grow our own vegetables.
Wir kaufen nicht viel Lebensmittel im Bioladen. Aber unser eigenes Gemüse bauen wir an.
I **did** know they were planning a new supermarket. But I *hadn't* realized it would be built this year.
Ich wußte natürlich schon ... Aber es war mir vorher nicht klar ...

Emphatic *do* is used especially in affirmative statements that are contrasted with negative statements.

Stressing a request

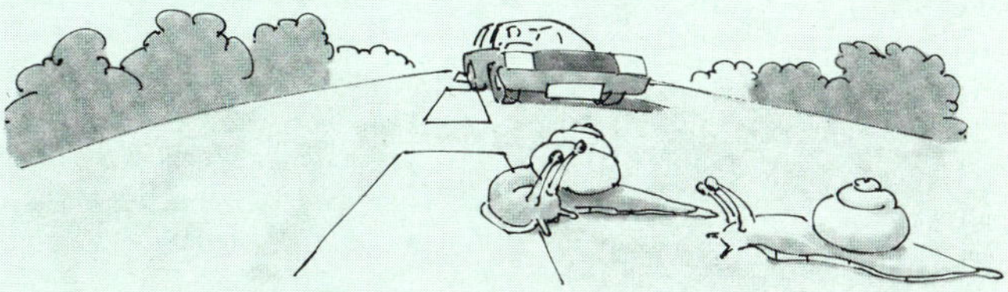

Do sit down. Setzen Sie sich doch bitte.

Do hurry up! Beeil dich doch!

Imperatives with emphatic *do* can express either extra politeness or impatience, depending on the context.

1 I **do** like this bread. Did you make it yourself? — Dieses Brot schmeckt aber gut.
I **did** enjoy the party. It was great to see you again. — Ich fand die Party wirklich toll.

Emphatic *do* is also used to express a spontaneous feeling or an emotional reaction.

2 You **are** [ˈɑː] working hard. Aren't you ready for a break yet? — Du arbeitest aber hart.

To give emphasis to sentences containing auxiliaries, the auxiliary itself is stressed.

9 Inversion as a stylistic device

Subject – verb – object is the usual word order in an English sentence. In some cases, however, it is possible to change the word order; this has a special stylistic effect.

Adverbial	Auxiliary	Subject	Main verb	Rest of the sentence
Hardly	**had**	**he**	**parked**	the car ***when*** he saw a traffic warden coming towards him.
No sooner	**had**	**we**	**left**	the main road ***than*** we realized we had taken the wrong turning.
Never in my life	**have**	**I**	**had**	such a rough crossing.
Not only	**did**	**the passengers**	**feel**	ill, ***but*** most of the crew were seasick, too.

If the sentence begins with a negative or restricting adverbial, the subject comes after the auxiliary – as in questions. This is called inversion.
If there is no auxiliary in the sentence, a form of *do* is used (as in the last example).

The following negative and restricting adverbials can be used in this way:

hardly (... when ...)	kaum (... als ...)	*never*	noch nie, niemals
scarcely (... when ...)	kaum (... als ...)	*seldom/rarely*	selten, kaum
no sooner (... than ...)	kaum (... als ...)	*neither ... nor ...*	weder ... noch ...
not only (... but ...)	nicht nur (... sondern ...)	(see also § 144)	

This word order is used mainly in formal style. In colloquial English, the usual word order – with the adverbial in mid position – is normally preferred (see also § 50):
He had hardly parked *the car when he saw the traffic warden coming towards him.*

Not until she got out of the car **did she see** how much damage had been done. — Erst als sie ausstieg, sah sie ...

An adverbial clause starting with *not until* is also followed by the inversion of auxiliary and subject (in the main clause).

Chapter 18: Reported speech (Indirect speech)

§ 150 The main characteristics of reported speech

Instead of quoting the original sentences word for word, it is normal to use reported speech to retell what somebody has said. Reported speech is usually formed with an introductory clause containing a verb such as *say, tell,* etc., followed by a *that*-clause. (See § 152 for reported questions and commands.)

Remember:
- No comma is used before the *that*-clause.
- *That* is often left out: *He says (that) he's broken his leg.*
- Personal pronouns, possessive determiners, etc. must be changed to fit the point of view of the person reporting (*I* → *he/she*, *my* → *his/her*, etc.). (For the shift of expressions of time and place, see § 153.)

To give an immediate report of what somebody has said (on the telephone, for example), it is natural to use an introductory clause in the present tense (e. g. *he says*).
The tenses that were used in direct speech then remain unchanged. In German the subjunctive is often used: *Er sagt, er* ***könne*** *nicht ... kommen. Er sagt, er* ***habe*** *sich das Bein gebrochen.*

When the report is given later, it is natural to use an introductory clause in the past tense (e. g. *he said*). In this case, the tenses that were used in direct speech must be shifted back (*can't come* → *couldn't come*, etc., see § 151).

⚠

She **said (to me)**	that she would be back late.	Sie **sagte (zu mir)** ...
She **told me**	that she would be back late.	Sie **sagte (zu) mir** ...

Say can take an indirect (personal) object. If it does, *to* must be used before this object.
Tell must always be followed by an indirect (personal) object, but without *to*.

N Brian *has told* me that he **can't come** to the party. He **has broken** his leg.

If the introductory clause is in the present perfect, the tenses that were used in direct speech remain unchanged (as they do after an introductory clause in the present tense).

Everybody missed Brian. A few hours before the party he *had told* Sue that he **couldn't come** because he **had broken** his leg.

If the introductory clause is in the past perfect, the tenses change as they do after an introductory clause in the past tense.

51 The backshift of tenses in reported speech

If the clause introducing reported speech is in the past tense (e. g. *he said, she told me,* etc.), the tenses that were used in direct speech are shifted back in the following way:

Direct speech	Reported speech (introductory clause in the past tense)
(From an interview with Debra Adams, a Newcastle schoolgirl.) '**I'm** in the school tennis team. I **love** sports! But **I'm working** for exams at the moment, so I **don't have** much time for tennis.'	Debra said that she **was** in the school tennis team. She said she **loved** sports. But she told me that she **was working** for exams at the moment. She said she **didn't have** much time for tennis.
present tense →	**past tense**
'**I've been** at Burnside School for five years. My boyfriend **has** already **left** school.'	She said she **had been** at Burnside School for five years. She told me that her boyfriend **had** already **left** school.
present perfect →	**past perfect**
'He **started** work as soon as he **left.** He **didn't** even **have** a summer holiday!'	She went on to say that he **had started** work as soon as he **had left.** She said he **hadn't** even **had** a summer holiday.
past tense →	**past perfect**
'**I'll** probably **leave** school at the end of the year. But I **won't give** up tennis!'	She told me that she **would** probably **leave** school at the end of the year. But she said she **wouldn't give** up tennis.
***will*-future** →	**conditional**
'I hope I **can** get a job at a bank, or at the post office. But finding work **may** be a bit of a problem.'	She said she hoped she **could** get a job at a bank or at the post office. But she thought that finding work **might** be a bit of a problem.
can → ***may*** →	***could*** ***might***

1 'I **hadn't expected** to get such a good seat.'
'I **would like** to be a film star –
but there's not much chance of that!'

He said he **hadn't expected** to get such a good seat.
She said she **would like** to be a film star ...

As the past perfect cannot be shifted back, it remains unchanged in reported speech. *Would, should, could* and *might* also remain unchanged.

2 'School in Germany **starts** at 8 o'clock or earlier.'
'Where I **come** from, the sun **doesn't set** in the
summer at all.'

Reinhard told me that school in Germany **starts** at ...
Brit told us that where she **comes** from,
the sun **doesn't set** in the summer at all.

The simple present can remain unchanged in reported speech to emphasize that something is always the case (e. g. habits that do not change, typical qualities, laws of nature).

§ 152 Questions and commands in reported speech

1. Reported questions (Indirect questions)

Direct speech	Reported speech
'**Do** you **speak** Spanish?'	→ Carol asked me ***if/whether*** I **spoke** Spanish.
'**Did** you **learn** it at school?'	→ Then she asked me ***if*** I **had learned** it at school.
'**Can** you **translate** the instructions for me?'	→ I asked my French teacher ***whether*** he **could translate** the instructions for me.

If the question in direct speech is formed without an interrogative (i. e. if it is a *yes/no*-question), *if* or *whether* is used to introduce the clause in reported speech.
(See § 140 for *yes/no*-questions.)

Direct speech	Reported speech
'***What*** **do** you **think** of my new CD player?'	→ Chris asked us ***what*** we **thought** of his new CD player.
'***When*** **did** you **buy** it?'	→ I asked him ***when*** he **had bought** it.
'***Where*** **have** you **put** your old record player?'	→ Sam asked him ***where*** he **had put** his old record player.

If the question in direct speech is introduced by an interrogative (*what, where, why, when, how,* etc.), this interrogative is used to introduce the clause in reported speech.
(See § 141 for questions with interrogatives.)

⚠ Direct speech: '**Can** you **swim**?' — 'Where **do** you **live**?'
Reported speech: He asked me if I **could swim.** — He asked me where I **lived.**

The word order in direct questions is *auxiliary – subject – main verb* (see § 140–141). But in reported questions, the word order is the same as in statements: *subject – (auxiliary) – main verb.*

N '***Where*** **shall** I **sign** my name?'
→ I had to ask ***where*** **to sign** my name.
(... ***where*** I **should sign** my name.)

It is sometimes possible to shorten a reported question containing a modal auxiliary by turning it into a construction with interrogative + infinitive. (See § 107.)

'I told you not to go so fast round the corners.'

2. Reported commands (Indirect commands)

Direct speech	Reported speech
'**Look** in the mirror before giving a signal.'	→ My driving instructor told me **to look** in the mirror before giving a signal.
'**Don't brake** too suddenly.'	→ He told me **not to brake** too suddenly.
'**Drive** extra carefully near schools and playgrounds.'	→ He also advised me **to drive** extra carefully near schools and playgrounds.

It is usual to express commands (imperatives) in reported speech by using the infinitive with *to.* For negative commands, *not* + infinitive with *to* is used. (See § 139 for affirmative and negative imperatives.)
The alternative construction, formed with a *that*-clause and *should,* is not so commonly used:
*He said **that** I **should drive** extra carefully near schools and playgrounds.*

N 'Hello, Mark. What about a game of tennis?'	I said hello to Mark and suggested a game of tennis.
'Oh, no. Later, perhaps.'	Mark didn't want to play, but said he might do so later.
'O.K. It's a bit too hot at the moment, isn't it?'	So I agreed and said it was a bit too hot at the moment.

To express greetings, exclamations and similar incomplete sentences in reported speech, it is usual to rephrase them or make them into whole sentences. Question tags are left out.

3 The shift of expressions of time and place in reported speech

Expressions of time such as *today, yesterday, this week* and expressions of place such as *here, there, in this country,* are naturally chosen to fit the point of view of the speaker (e.g. *today* = the day on which the speaker is talking; *here* = the place where the speaker is talking).
In reported speech, these expressions of time and place have to fit the point of view of the person reporting. Because of this, they must often be changed. (See § 150 for the shift of personal pronouns.)

1. Expressions of time

Direct speech	**Reported speech**	
	Period of time not yet over	**Period of time over**
Friday 13th	**Friday 13th**	**A few days later**

Weatherman on TV:	Mr Brown to Mrs Brown:	Mrs Brown to Mr Brown:
'The rain will stop **tomorrow.**'	'The weatherman said the rain would stop **tomorrow.**'	'Don't you remember, dear? On Friday the weatherman said the rain would stop **the next day / on Saturday.**'

Expressions of time such as *yesterday, today, this month, next year,* etc. remain unchanged if the report is given before that particular day, month, year, etc. is over.
But if that particular period of time is already over when the report is given, expressions of time are changed as follows:

today	→ **that** day	yesterday	→ **the** day **before**	tomorrow	→ **the next** day/ **the following** day
tonight	→ **that** night	**last** Friday	→ **the** Friday **before**		
this week	→ **that** week	**last** month	→ **the** month **before**	**next** year	→ **the next** year/ **the following** year
this year	→ **that** year	two days **ago**	→ two days **before**		

Instead of shifting the expressions of time, it is also possible to name the particular day, month, year, etc. (e.g. *on Saturday).*

2. Expressions of place

Direct speech	Reported speech	
	Report given from the same place	Report given from a different place
Prime Minister (in Britain):	**Newsreader on British TV**	**Newsreader on American TV**
'More will have to be done **in this country** to protect the environment. Industries **here** will play a leading role.'	'The Prime Minister said that more would have to be done **in this country** to protect the environment, and that industries **here** would play a leading role.'	'The British Prime Minister said that more would have to be done **in Britain** to protect the environment, and that industries **there** would play a leading role.'

Expressions of place such as *here, in this country,* etc. can remain unchanged if someone gives a report from the same place as the original speaker.
If this is not the case, the name of the place, or an exact description of it, is usually given. If it is clear from the context what place is meant, expressions such as *there, in that country,* etc. can be used.

Appendix

1 Irregular verbs

Infinitive	Past tense	Past participle	
be [i:]	was/were	been [i:]	*sein*
bear [eə]	bore [ɔ:]	born(e) [ɔ:]	*(er)tragen, gebären*
beat [i:]	beat [i:]	beaten [i:]	*schlagen*
become [ʌ]	became [eɪ]	become [ʌ]	*werden*
begin [ɪ]	began [æ]	begun [ʌ]	*anfangen*
bet [e]	bet [e]*	bet [e]*	*wetten*
bind [aɪ]	bound [aʊ]	bound [aʊ]	*binden*
bite [aɪ]	bit [ɪ]	bit(ten) [ɪ]	*beißen*
bleed [i:]	bled [e]	bled [e]	*bluten*
blow [əʊ]	blew [u:]	blown [əʊ]	*blasen*
break [eɪ]	broke [əʊ]	broken [əʊ]	*(zer)brechen*
bring [ɪ]	brought [ɔ:]	brought [ɔ:]	*(her)bringen*
build [ɪ]	built [ɪ]	built [ɪ]	*bauen*
burn [ɜ:]	burnt [ɜ:]*	burnt [ɜ:]*	*(ver)brennen*
burst [ɜ:]	burst [ɜ:]	burst [ɜ:]	*platzen*
buy [aɪ]	bought [ɔ:]	bought [ɔ:]	*kaufen*
catch [æ]	caught [ɔ:]	caught [ɔ:]	*fangen*
choose [u:]	chose [əʊ]	chosen [əʊ]	*(aus)wählen*
come [ʌ]	came [eɪ]	come [ʌ]	*kommen*
cost [ɒ]	cost [ɒ]	cost [ɒ]	*kosten*
cut [ʌ]	cut [ʌ]	cut [ʌ]	*schneiden*
deal [i:]	dealt [e]	dealt [e]	*handeln (von)*
dig [ɪ]	dug [ʌ]	dug [ʌ]	*graben*
do [u:]	did [ɪ]	done [ʌ]	*tun*
draw [ɔ:]	drew [u:]	drawn [ɔ:]	*zeichnen, ziehen*
dream [i:]	dreamt [e]*	dreamt [e]*	*träumen*
drink [ɪ]	drank [æ]	drunk [ʌ]	*trinken*
drive [aɪ]	drove [əʊ]	driven [ɪ]	*fahren*
eat [i:]	ate [e]/[eɪ]	eaten [i:]	*essen*
fall [ɔ:]	fell [e]	fallen [ɔ:]	*fallen*
feed [i:]	fed [e]	fed [e]	*füttern*
feel [i:]	felt [e]	felt [e]	*(sich) fühlen*
fight [aɪ]	fought [ɔ:]	fought [ɔ:]	*(be)kämpfen*
find [aɪ]	found [aʊ]	found [aʊ]	*finden*
flee [i:]	fled [e]	fled [e]	*fliehen*
fly [aɪ]	flew [u:]	flown [əʊ]	*fliegen*
forbid [ɪ]	forbade [æ]	forbidden [ɪ]	*verbieten*
forget [e]	forgot [ɒ]	forgotten [ɒ]	*vergessen*
forgive [ɪ]	forgave [eɪ]	forgiven [ɪ]	*verzeihen, vergeben*
freeze [i:]	froze [əʊ]	frozen [əʊ]	*(er)frieren*
get [e]	got [ɒ]	got [ɒ]	*bekommen, werden*
give [ɪ]	gave [eɪ]	given [ɪ]	*geben*
go [əʊ]	went [e]	gone [ɒ]	*gehen, fahren*
grow [əʊ]	grew [u:]	grown [əʊ]	*wachsen, anbauen*
hang [æ]	hung [ʌ]	hung [ʌ]	*(auf)hängen*
have [æ]	had [æ]	had [æ]	*haben*
hear [ɪə]	heard [ɜ:]	heard [ɜ:]	*hören*
hide [aɪ]	hid [ɪ]	hidden [ɪ]	*(sich) verstecken*

* The regular form ending in *-ed* is also used.

Infinitive	Past tense	Past participle	
hit [ɪ]	hit [ɪ]	hit [ɪ]	*schlagen, treffen*
hold [əʊ]	held [e]	held [e]	*halten*
hurt [ɜ:]	hurt [ɜ:]	hurt [ɜ:]	*verletzen, wehtun*
keep [i:]	kept [e]	kept [e]	*(be)halten*
know [nəʊ]	knew [nju:]	known [nəʊn]	*wissen, kennen*
lay [eɪ]	laid [eɪ]	laid [eɪ]	*legen*
lead [i:]	led [e]	led [e]	*führen, leiten*
lean [i:]	leant [e]*	leant [e]*	*lehnen*
learn [ɜ:]	learnt [ɜ:]*	learnt [ɜ:]*	*lernen*
leave [i:]	left [e]	left [e]	*(zurück-/ver-)lassen*
lend [e]	lent [e]	lent [e]	*leihen*
let [e]	let [e]	let [e]	*lassen*
lie [aɪ]	lay [eɪ]	lain [eɪ]	*liegen*
light [aɪ]	lit [ɪ]*	lit [ɪ]*	*beleuchten, anzünden*
lose [u:]	lost [ɒ]	lost [ɒ]	*verlieren*
make [eɪ]	made [eɪ]	made [eɪ]	*machen*
mean [i:]	meant [e]	meant [e]	*meinen, bedeuten*
meet [i:]	met [e]	met [e]	*(sich) treffen*
pay [eɪ]	paid [eɪ]	paid [eɪ]	*bezahlen*
put [ʊ]	put [ʊ]	put [ʊ]	*legen, setzen, stellen*
read [i:]	read [e]	read [e]	*lesen*
ride [aɪ]	rode [əʊ]	ridden [ɪ]	*reiten, fahren*
ring [ɪ]	rang [æ]	rung [ʌ]	*läuten*
rise [aɪ]	rose [əʊ]	risen [ɪ]	*aufstehen, aufgehen*
run [ʌ]	ran [æ]	run [ʌ]	*laufen, rennen*
say [eɪ]	said [e]	said [e]	*sagen*
see [i:]	saw [ɔ:]	seen [i:]	*sehen*
seek [i:]	sought [ɔ:]	sought [ɔ:]	*suchen*
sell [e]	sold [əʊ]	sold [əʊ]	*verkaufen*
send [e]	sent [e]	sent [e]	*senden, schicken*
set [e]	set [e]	set [e]	*setzen, stellen*
sew [əʊ]	sewed [əʊ]	sewn [əʊ]*	*nähen*
shake [ei]	shook [ʊ]	shaken [eɪ]	*schütteln*
shine [aɪ]	shone [ɒ]	shone [ɒ]	*scheinen*
shoot [u:]	shot [ɒ]	shot [ɒ]	*schießen*
show [əʊ]	showed [əʊ]	shown [əʊ]	*zeigen*
shrink [ɪ]	shrank [æ]	shrunk [ʌ]	*schrumpfen, einlaufen*
shut [ʌ]	shut [ʌ]	shut [ʌ]	*schließen, zumachen*
sing [ɪ]	sang [æ]	sung [ʌ]	*singen*
sink [ɪ]	sank [æ]	sunk [ʌ]	*sinken, versenken*
sit [ɪ]	sat [æ]	sat [æ]	*sitzen, sich setzen*
sleep [i:]	slept [e]	slept [e]	*schlafen*
smell [e]	smelt [e]	smelt [e]	*riechen*
sow [əʊ]	sowed [əʊ]	sown [əʊ]	*säen*
speak [i:]	spoke [əʊ]	spoken [əʊ]	*sprechen*
spell [e]	spelt [e]*	spelt [e]*	*buchstabieren*
spend [e]	spent [e]	spent [e]	*verbringen, ausgeben*
spill [ɪ]	spilt [ɪ]*	spilt [ɪ]*	*vergießen, verschütten*
split [ɪ]	split [ɪ]	split [ɪ]	*(zer)teilen, spalten*
spoil [ɔɪ]	spoilt [ɔɪ]*	spoilt [ɔɪ]*	*verderben*
spread [e]	spread [e]	spread [e]	*(sich) ausbreiten*
spring [ɪ]	sprang [æ]	sprung [ʌ]	*springen*
stand [æ]	stood [ʊ]	stood [ʊ]	*stehen*
steal [i:]	stole [əʊ]	stolen [əʊ]	*stehlen*
stick [ɪ]	stuck [ʌ]	stuck [ʌ]	*kleben*

* The regular form ending in *-ed* is also used.

Infinitive	Past tense	Past participle	
strike [aɪ]	struck [ʌ]	struck [ʌ]	*stoßen, schlagen*
swear [eə]	swore [ɔ:]	sworn [ɔ:]	*schwören, fluchen*
sweep [i:]	swept [e]	swept [e]	*fegen*
swim [ɪ]	swam [æ]	swum [ʌ]	*schwimmen*
swing [ɪ]	swung [ʌ]	swung [ʌ]	*schwingen, schaukeln*
take [eɪ]	took [ʊ]	taken [eɪ]	*nehmen, (hin)bringen*
teach [i:]	taught [ɔ:]	taught [ɔ:]	*lehren, unterrichten*
tear [eə]	tore [ɔ:]	torn [ɔ:]	*reißen*
tell [e]	told [əʊ]	told [əʊ]	*erzählen, sagen*
think [ɪ]	thought [ɔ:]	thought [ɔ:]	*denken, glauben*
throw [əʊ]	threw [u:]	thrown [əʊ]	*werfen*
understand [æ]	understood [ʊ]	understood [ʊ]	*verstehen*
wake [eɪ]	woke [əʊ]*	woken [əʊ]*	*wecken, aufwachen*
wear [eə]	wore [ɔ:]	worn [ɔ:]	*tragen (Kleidung)*
win [ɪ]	won [ʌ]	won [ʌ]	*gewinnen*
write [aɪ]	wrote [əʊ]	written [ɪ]	*schreiben*

* The regular form ending in *-ed* is also used.

2 Table of tenses: active and passive voice

		Active	**Passive**
Present tense	simple	Judy **takes** Sammy for a walk every afternoon.	The dog **is taken** for walks regularly.
	progressive	Judy **is taking** Sammy for a walk.	Sammy **is being taken** to the vet's now.
Past tense	simple	Last summer Mark **took** lots of photos.	This photo **was taken** two years ago.
	progressive	Someone walked in front of the camera while Mark **was taking** a photo.	Unfortunately the light got in while the film **was being taken** out of the camera.
Present perfect	simple	Dad **has taken** the boys to school in the car.	Judy **has been taken** to hospital. She is seriously ill.
	progressive	Paul **has been taking** driving lessons for nearly three months now.	–
Past perfect	simple	Dad went to the office after he **had taken** the boys to school.	Mark didn't eat much for a day or two after his tooth **had been taken** out.
	progressive	Paul was afraid of failing his driving test, although he **had been taking** lessons for months.	–
Will-future	simple	Sarah's training as a vet **will take** six years.	A photograph of the school-leavers **will be taken** outside the school hall next Monday.
	progressive	Next year at this time Judy **will be taking** her A-levels.	–
Future perfect	simple	Tomorrow at this time our plane **will have taken** off.	Our luggage **will have been taken** on board long before the flight is called.
	progressive	John is learning to fly. By the end of this year he **will have been taking** lessons for six months.	–
Conditional	simple	If Mark had a dog, he **would take** it out regularly.	If Judy was serously ill, she **would be taken** to hospital at once.
	progressive	If the weather wasn't so terrible, Judy **would be taking** Sammy for a walk now.	–
Conditional perfect	simple	If Mum had known that Judy felt ill, she **would have taken** her to the doctor's.	If Judy had been seriously ill, she **would have been taken** to hospital at once.
	progressive	If Mark hadn't been ill all winter, he **would have been taking** his exams in June.	–

3 Word formation

Word formation is the formation of new words from already existing ones. This is often done by adding prefixes or suffixes, for example. With an understanding of the basic principles of word formation, it is possible to make out the meaning of a great number of apparently new words.

1. The addition of prefixes

	Meanings	Noun	Verb	Adjective	
re-	'again', 'back',		to **re**write		neu schreiben
		repayment	to **re**pay	**re**payable	Rückzahlung, zurückzahlen, rückzahlbar
in- (***im-*** before *b, p, m,* ***il-*** before *l,* ***ir-*** before *r*)	'not', 'opposite of'	**in**action		**in**active	Untätigkeit, untätig
		independence		**in**dependent	Unabhängigkeit, unabhängig
		impossibility		**im**possible	Unmöglichkeit, unmöglich
		illogicality		**il**logical	Unlogik, unlogisch
		irregularity		**ir**regular	Unregelmäßigkeit, unregelmäßig
un-	'not', 'opposite of', 'reverse'	**un**happiness		**un**happy	Traurigkeit, unglücklich
		uncertainty		**un**certain	Ungewißheit, ungewiß
			to **un**lock	**un**locked	aufschließen, unverschlossen
dis-		**dis**honesty		**dis**honest	Unehrlichkeit, unehrlich
		disappearance	to **dis**appear		das Verschwinden, verschwinden
		disqualification	to **dis**qualify		Disqualifizierung, disqualifizieren
			to **dis**connect	**dis**connected	unterbrechen, unzusammenhängend
de-	'reverse' or 'take away'	**de**forestation	to **de**forest		Abholzung, abholzen
mis-	'wrong'	**mis**understanding	to **mis**understand		Mißverständnis, mißverstehen
			to **mis**lead	**mis**leading	irreführen, irreführend
mal-	'bad'	**mal**treatment	to **mal**treat	**mal**treated	Mißhandlung, mißhandeln, mißhandelt
over-	'too much'	**over**crowding	to **over**crowd	**over**crowded	Überfüllung, überfüllen, überfüllt
under-	'not enough', 'too little'	**under**payment	to **under**pay	**under**paid	Unterbezahlung, unterbezahlen, unterbezahlt
super-	'over', 'more than'			**super**human	übermenschlich
sub-	'under', 'less than'	**sub**way			Unterführung (BE), U-Bahn (AE)
				subnormal	minderbegabt
inter-	'between', 'among'	**inter**action	to **inter**act		Wechselwirkung, aufeinander wirken
				international	international
co-	'together'	**co**-operation	to **co**-operate	**co**-operative	Zusammenarbeit, zusammenarbeiten, hilfsbereit

Prefix	Meaning	Noun	Verb	Adjective	German
pre-	'before' (time)	**pre**history		**pre**historic	Vorgeschichte, vorgeschichtlich
			to **pre**heat		vorheizen
post-	'after' (time)			**post**war	Nachkriegs-
trans-	'across', 'over'			**trans**atlantic	transatlantisch
		transplant(ation)	to **trans**plant		Verpflanzung, verpflanzen
pro-	'for' (attitude)			**pro-**American	proamerikanisch
anti-	'against' (effect or attitude)	**anti**freeze			Frostschutz
				anti-American	antiamerikanisch
counter	'against' (direction or reaction)	**counter-**attack	to **counter-**attack		Gegenangriff, einen Gegenangriff starten

2. The addition of suffixes

Rule	Noun	Verb	Adjective	German
Adjective + ***-ness / -(i)ty / -ence / -th*** → **Noun** (quality or state)	dark**ness** ←		dark	Dunkelheit
	activ**ity**		active	Aktivität
	certain**ty**		certain	Gewißheit
	differ**ence**		different	Unterschied
	tru**th**		true	Wahrheit
	leng**th**		long	Länge
Verb + ***-ment / -ion / -ation / -ision*** → **Noun** (activity or process)	move**ment** ←	to move		Bewegung
	act**ion**	to act		Handlung
	examin**ation**	to examine		Prüfung
	dec**ision**	to decide		Entscheidung
Verb + ***-er / -or*** → **Noun** (person that does s.th.; tool or machine)	writ**er** ←	to write		Schriftsteller(in)
	act**or**	to act		Schauspieler
	mix**er**	to mix		Mixer, Rührgerät
Verb + ***-ing*** → **Noun** (process or result)	begin**ning** ←	to begin		Anfang
	build**ing**	to build		Gebäude
Verb + ***-ing / -ed / -ive / -able / -ible*** → **Adjective**		to surprise →	surpris**ing**	überraschend
		to surprise	surpris**ed**	überrascht
		to create	creat**ive**	schöpferisch
		to understand	understand**able**	verständlich
		to divide	divis**ible**	teilbar
Noun + ***-ous / -al / -ic / -ical / -y / -ful / -less*** → **Adjective**	danger →		danger**ous**	gefährlich
	tradition		tradition**al**	traditionell
	artist		artist**ic**	künstlerisch
	type		typ**ical**	typisch
	dirt		dirt**y**	schmutzig
	beauty		beauti**ful**	schön
	power		power**less**	machtlos
Adjective + ***-en / -ize / -ify*** → **Verb**		to short**en** ←	short	kürzen
		to modern**ize**	modern	modernisieren
		to simpl**ify**	simple	vereinfachen

3. Conversion

A large number of English words are formed by conversion, i. e. when a word of a certain class (e. g. a noun: *rain*) is used in a different word class (e. g. as a verb: *to rain*).

Noun	Verb	Adjective	
the rain	to rain		Regen, regnen
an answer	to answer		Antwort, antworten
a surprise	to surprise		Überraschung, überraschen
	to dry	dry	trocknen, trocken
	to empty	empty	leeren, leer
an equal	to equal	equal	Gleichgestellte(r), gleichen, gleich
a giant		giant	Riese, riesig
a secret		secret	Geheimnis, geheim
a sweet		sweet	Bonbon, süß

4. Compounds

It is also possible to form new words by joining two words together. Some of these compounds are written as two separate words, but most of them are written either with a hyphen or as one word.

Most compounds are compound nouns.

apple tree	Apfelbaum	dining-room	Eßzimmer
car park	Parkplatz	freeway	Autobahn (AE)
dishwasher	Spülmaschine	redwood	(Baumart)
postman	Postbote	wildlife	Tierwelt
boyfriend	Freund	Outback	(australisches Hinterland)
earthquake	Erdbeben		
washing-machine	Waschmaschine	underground	U-Bahn (BE)

There are also compound adjectives. Many of these are formed with present or past participles (e. g. *good-looking, man-made*), or with a noun + *-ed* (e. g. *empty-handed*).

bitter-sweet	bittersüß	good-looking	gutaussehend
dark blue	dunkelblau	everlasting	immerwährend
second-best	zweitbeste(r/s)	heartbreaking	herzzerbrechend
duty-free	zollfrei	man-made	künstlich (hergestellt)
seasick	seekrank		
waterproof	wasserdicht	empty-handed	mit leeren Händen
fair-haired	blond	narrow-minded	engstirnig

New words can also be formed by

– shortening existing words:
- advertisement [əd'vɜ:tɪsmənt] → advert, ad ['ædvɜ:t], [æd]
- examination → exam
- laboratory [lə'bɒrətrɪ] → lab [læb]
- mathematics → maths

– mixing words:
- smoke + fog → smog
- breakfast + lunch → brunch

– using initials (the first letters of words):
- very important person → VIP [ˌvi:aɪ'pi:]
- Member of Parliament → MP [ˌem'pi:]
- United Nations International Children's Emergency Fund → UNICEF ['ju:nɪsef]

4 Phonetic symbols

Short vowels	Long vowels	Diphthongs	Voiceless consonants	Voiced consonants	
[ɪ] sit	[iː] see	[eɪ] name	[s] sun	[z] easy	[l] land
[ʌ] cut	[ɑː] ask	[aɪ] time	[ʃ] ship	[ʒ] vision	[m] man
[ɒ] box	[ɔː] broad	[ɔɪ] boy	[tʃ] chin	[dʒ] Jim	[n] neck
[ʊ] put	[uː] moon	[əʊ] cold	[θ] thin	[ð] then	[ŋ] long
[e] let	[ɜː] bird	[aʊ] house	[f] fan	[v] van	[r] red
[æ] hat		[ɪə] here	[p] pig	[b] big	[h] hand
[ə] another		[eə] chair	[t] town	[d] down	[j] yes
		[ʊə] sure	[k] car	[g] gas	[w] water

Stress marks

kangaroo [ˌkæŋɡəˈruː]	ˈ = main stress	ˌ = secondary stress
copilot [ˈ–ˌ––]	– marks a syllable (when only stress, not pronunciation, is shown).	

5 The English alphabet

a	b	c	d	e	f	g	h	i	j	k	l	m	n
[eɪ]	[biː]	[siː]	[diː]	[iː]	[ef]	[dʒiː]	[eɪtʃ]	[aɪ]	[dʒeɪ]	[keɪ]	[el]	[em]	[en]
o	p	q	r	s	t	u	v	w	x	y	z		
[əʊ]	[piː]	[kjuː]	[ɑː]	[es]	[tiː]	[juː]	[viː]	[ˈdʌbljuː]	[eks]	[waɪ]	BE [zed], AE [ziː]		

6 English terms for punctuation marks

.	BE: full stop, AE: period [ˈpɪərɪəd]	-	hyphen [ˈhaɪfən] *(Bindestrich)*
,	comma	" " ' '	inverted commas, (double/single) quotation marks
;	semi-colon [ˌsemɪˈkəʊlən]	'	apostrophe [əˈpɒstrəfɪ]
:	colon	( )	(round) brackets
?	question mark	[ ]	square brackets
!	exclamation mark [ˌekskləˈmeɪʃn]	/	stroke
–	dash *(Gedankenstrich)*		

7 English-German list of grammatical terms

active voice ['æktɪv 'vɔɪs]	Aktiv	*The police arrested the thief.* (cf. passive voice)
activity verb [æk'tɪvətɪ ˌvɜ:b]	Tätigkeitsverb	*read, eat, walk, work,* etc.
adjective ['ædʒɪktɪv]	Adjektiv	*good, bad, terrible,* etc.
adverb ['ædvɜ:b]	Adverb	*well, badly, terribly, often, never,* etc.
adverb of comment ['kɒment]	kommentierendes Adverb	*luckily, unfortunately, obviously,* etc.
adverb of definite time ['defɪnɪt]	Adverb der bestimmten Zeit	*today, yesterday,* etc.
adverb of degree [dɪ'gri:]	Gradadverb	*very, quite, rather,* etc.
adverb of indefinite frequency [ɪn'defɪnɪt 'fri:kwensɪ]	Adverb der unbestimmten Häufigkeit	*always, often, sometimes,* etc.
adverb of indefinite time	Adverb der unbestimmten Zeit	*soon, already,* etc.
adverb of manner ['mænə]	Adverb der Art und Weise	*carefully, slowly, loudly,* etc.
adverb of place	Ortsadverb	*here, there, upstairs, somewhere,* etc.
adverbial (phrase) [əd'vɜ:bjəl 'freɪz]	adverbiale Bestimmung	*in the garden, two days ago, every day,* etc.
adverbial clause [klɔ:z]	adverbialer Nebensatz	I can't go out *because it's raining.*
affirmative statement [ə'fɜ:mətɪv 'steɪtmənt]	bejahter Aussagesatz	*That is true.* (cf. negative statement)
antecedent (of a relative clause) [ˌæntɪ'si:dnt]	Bezugswort (eines Relativsatzes)	*the person* who helped me *a story* that really happened
attributive use (of adjectives) [ə'trɪbjʊtɪv 'ju:s]	attributiver Gebrauch (von Adjektiven)	a *new* car (cf. predicative use)
auxiliary [ɔ:g'zɪljərɪ]	Hilfsverb	*be, have, do, can, may, must,* etc.
backshift of tenses (in reported speech) ['bækʃɪft]	Rückverschiebung der Zeitformen (in der indirekten Rede)	'I *can't* come.' → He said he *couldn't* come.
by-agent ['baɪ ˌeɪdʒnt]	–	The thief was arrested *by the police.*
cardinal numbers ['kɑ:dɪnl]	Grundzahlen	*one, two, three,* etc.(cf. ordinal numbers)
clause [klɔ:z]	Neben-/Hauptsatz	see main clause, subordinate clause
collective noun [kə'lektɪv]	Gruppenbezeichnung	*family, team, class, crew,* etc.
command [kə'mɑ:nd]	Aufforderungssatz	see imperative sentence
comparative [kəm'pærətɪv]	Komparativ	*better, faster, more expensive,* etc.
complement ['kɒmplɪmənt]	(Verb-)Ergänzung	She is *a Catholic.* He remained *silent.*
comparison [kəm'pærɪsn]	Steigerung	good – *better – best;* expensive – *more expensive – most expensive*
compound ['kɒmpaʊnd]	Zusammensetzung	*school uniform, record-player, cowboy,* etc.
conditional [kən'dɪʃənl]	–	I *would work* harder.
conditional perfect ['pɜ:fekt]	–	I *would have worked* harder.
conditional sentence	Bedingungssatzgefüge	*If it rains, we'll stay at home.*
conjunction [kən'dʒʌŋkʃn]	Konjunktion	*while, because, though, if,* etc.
contact clause ['kɒntækt ˌklɔ:z]	Relativsatz ohne Relativpronomen	The book *I'm reading* is fantastic.
countable noun ['kaʊntəbl]	zählbares Nomen	a *book* – two books (cf. uncountable noun)
defining relative clause [dɪ'faɪnɪŋ 'relətɪv 'klɔ:z]	notwendiger Relativsatz	The waitress *who served us yesterday* was very friendly. (cf. non-defining relative clause)
definite article ['defɪnɪt 'ɑ:tɪkl]	bestimmter Artikel	*the*
demonstrative determiner [dɪ'mɒnstrətɪv dɪ'tɜ:mɪnə]	Demonstrativbegleiter	*this* book, *that* house, *these* magazines, *those* people
demonstrative pronoun ['prəʊnaʊn]	Demonstrativpronomen	*This* is our house. What's *that? These* are my books, and *those* are yours.

* cf. = compare

direct object ['daɪrekt 'ɒbdʒekt]	direktes Objekt	He gave me *a book.* (cf. indirect object)
direct speech ['daɪrekt 'spi:tʃ]	direkte Rede	*'I can't come,'* he said. (cf. reported speech)
dynamic verb [daɪ'næmik 'vɜ:b]	Verb, bei dem die *progressive form* möglich ist	*read, walk, eat, work, become, grow,* etc. (cf. stative verb)
emphatic use of *do* [ɪm'fætɪk 'ju:s]	Hervorhebung mit *do*	I'm not very keen on sports, but I *do* like swimming.
expression of quantity [ɪk'spreʃn əv 'kwɒntɪtɪ]	Mengenangabe	*a piece of* cake, *two pounds of* apples, *some* salt
expression of frequency ['fri:kwənsɪ]	Wiederholungszahl	*once, twice, three times,* etc.
expression of place	Ortsangabe	*in front of the house, at the table,* etc.
expression of time	Zeitangabe	*in the morning, on Friday,* etc.
future ['fju:tʃə]	–	see *will*-future
future perfect [ˌfju:tʃə 'pɜ:fekt]	–	I *will have finished* the job soon.
general personal pronoun ['dʒenrl ˌpɜ:sənl 'prəʊnaʊn]	allgemeines Personalpronomen –	*One* shouldn't change *one's* mind too often. *You* never know what may happen.
gerund ['dʒerənd]	–	I like *playing* tennis. *Dancing* is fun.
going to-future		They *are going to move* to Exeter.
if-clause ['ɪf ˌklɔ:z]	*if*-Satz	I'll come with you *if I have time.*
imperative [ɪm'perətɪv]	Imperativ	*Come* in. *Don't wait* outside.
imperative sentence	Aufforderungssatz	*Come in. Don't wait outside.*
indefinite article [ɪn'defɪnɪt 'ɑ:tɪkl]	unbestimmter Artikel	*a, an*
indefinite determiner [dɪ'tɜ:mɪnə]	unbestimmter Begleiter	*some* butter, (not) *any* milk, (not) *many* people, etc.
indefinite pronoun ['prəʊnaʊn]	unbestimmtes Pronomen	*someone, anything, everybody, nothing,* etc.
indirect object ['ɪndaɪˌrekt 'ɒbdʒekt]	indirektes Objekt	He gave *me* a book. The teacher explained the problem *to the pupils.* (cf. direct object)
indirect question	indirekter Fragesatz	They asked me *where I lived.*
indirect speech	indirekte Rede	see reported speech
infinitive [ɪn'fɪnətɪv]	Infinitiv	*(to) be, (to) do, (to) work,* etc.
interrogative [ˌɪntə'rɒgətɪv]	Fragewort	*how, why, where, when,* etc.
introductory verb (in reported speech) [ˌɪntrə'dʌktərɪ 'vɜ:b]	einführendes Verb (bei der indirekten Rede)	He *said* he couldn't come. She *told* me she had passed her exam.
inversion [ɪn'vɜ:ʃn]	Inversion (Umstellung von Subjekt und Hilfsverb)	Never *have I seen* such a crowd.
irregular verb [ɪ'regjʊlə]	unregelmäßiges Verb	*go – went – gone* (cf. regular verb)
main clause ['meɪn 'klɔ:z]	Hauptsatz	*We'll ring you up* as soon as we arrive.
main verb	Vollverb	*go, read, know,* etc. (cf. auxiliary verb)
modal auxiliary ['məʊdl ɔ:g'zɪljərɪ]	modales Hilfsverb	*can, may, must, shall, will,* etc.
negative statement ['negətɪv 'steɪtmənt]	verneinter Aussagesatz	*That isn't true.* (cf. affirmative statement)
non-defining relative clause ['nɒn dɪ'faɪnɪŋ 'relətɪv 'klɔ:z]	nicht-notwendiger Relativsatz	Captain Cook, *who was born in Yorkshire,* was a famous explorer. (cf. defining relative clause)
notional subject ['nəʊʃənl]	Sinnsubjekt	There's *a fly* in my soup.
noun [naʊn]	Nomen, Substantiv	*book, water, music, people,* etc.
numbers	Zahlen	see cardinal numbers, ordinal numbers
object ['ɒbdʒekt]	Objekt	see direct object, indirect object
of-phrase ['ɒv freɪz]	–	the roof *of the house,* the end *of the road*
ordinal numbers ['ɔ:dɪnl]	Ordnungszahlen	*first, second, third,* etc.
participle ['pɑ:tɪsɪpl]	Partizip	see present participle, past participle

particle ['pɑ:tɪkl]	(Adverbial-)Partikel	take *off,* go *in,* pick *up,* etc.
passive infinitive ['pæsɪv ɪn'fɪnətɪv]	Passivform des Infinitivs	*(to) be discovered, (to) be repaired,* etc.
passive voice ['pæsɪv 'vɔɪs]	Passiv	*The thief was arrested (by the police).* (cf. active voice)
past participle ['pɑ:st 'pɑ:tɪsɪpl]	–	a *damaged* car, a play *written* by Shakespeare (cf. present participle)
past perfect ['pɑ:st 'pɜ:fekt]	–	We *had finished* our meal before he arrived.
past tense ['pɑ:st 'tens]	–	She *opened* the door and *went* out.
personal pronoun ['pɜ:sənl 'prəʊnaʊn]	Personalpronomen	*I, you, he, she,* etc.
phrasal verb ['freɪzl 'vɜ:b]	–	*take off, give up, put on,* etc.
plural ['plʊərəl]	Plural (Mehrzahl)	some *books,* two *magazines* (cf. singular)
possessive determiner [pə'zesɪv dɪ'tɜ:mɪnə]	Possessivbegleiter	*my* coat, *your* anorak, *his* scarf, etc.
possessive pronoun ['prəʊnaʊn]	Possessivpronomen	*mine, yours, his, hers,* etc.
predicative use (of adjectives) [prɪ'dɪkətɪv 'ju:s]	prädikativer Gebrauch (von Adjektiven)	This car is *new.* (cf. attributive use)
prefix ['pri:fɪks]	Vorsilbe	*un*happy, *dis*advantage, *re*open, etc.
preposition [ˌprepə'zɪʃn]	Präposition	*in* the house, *at* the table, *for* a friend
present participle ['preznt 'pɑ:tɪsɪpl]	–	a *sleeping* child, a family *living* in Dover (cf. past participle)
present perfect ['pɜ:fekt]	–	I *have finished* the job now.
present tense [tens]	–	She *works* in an office.
process verb ['prəʊses ˌvɜ:b]	Vorgangsverb	*become, grow, get,* etc.
progressive form [prə'gresɪv 'fɔ:m]	–	He *is/was/has been/had been working,* etc. (cf. simple form)
proper name [neɪm]	Eigenname	*Carol, Mr Brown, London, the Thames,* etc.
prop-word ['prɒp ˌwɜ:d]	Stützwort	a white shirt, a green *one* and two blue *ones*
question tag ['kwestʃn ˌtæg]	Bestätigungsfrage	It's a lovely day, *isn't it?*
question word	Fragewort	*how, why, where, when,* etc.
reciprocal pronoun [rɪ'sɪprəkl 'prəʊnaʊn]	reziprokes Pronomen	*each other, one another*
reflexive pronoun [rɪ'fleksɪv]	Reflexivpronomen (rückbezügliches Pronomen)	She introduced *herself.* We made *ourselves* some tea.
regular verb ['regjʊlə 'vɜ:b]	regelmäßiges Verb	*arrive – arrived* (cf. irregular verb)
relative clause ['relətɪv 'klɔ:z]	Relativsatz	see defining relative clause, contact clause, non-defining relative clause
relative pronoun	Relativpronomen	the man *who/that* helped me, a story *which/that* really happened
reported speech (indirect speech) [rɪ'pɔ:tɪd 'spi:tʃ]	indirekte Rede	He said *(that) he couldn't come.* (cf. direct speech)
s-genitive ['es 'dʒenɪtɪv]	*s*-Genitiv	*Bob's* bike, *my parents'* car
sentence ['sentəns]	Satz	
sentence pattern ['pætən]	Satzmuster	
short answer ['ʃɔ:t 'ɑ:nsə]	Kurzantwort	Do you like milk? – *Yes, I do./No, I don't.*
short(ened) sentence	Kurzsatz	I don't like fish. – *Nor do I./I do.*
sibilant ['sɪbɪlənt]	Zischlaut	[s, z, ʃ, ʒ, tʃ, dʒ]
simple form ['sɪmpl 'fɔ:m]	–	He *works/worked/has worked/had worked,* etc. (cf. progressive form)
singular ['sɪŋgjʊlə]	Singular (Einzahl)	a *book,* a *magazine,* etc. (cf. plural)
speech intention ['spi:tʃ ɪn'tenʃn]	Sprechabsicht	
statement ['steɪtmənt]	Aussage(satz)	see affirmative statement, negative statement
stative verb ['stætɪv 'vɜ:b]	Verb, bei dem die *progressive form* nicht möglich ist	*know, love, seem, belong,* etc. (cf. dynamic verb)

stylistic device [staɪˈlɪstɪk dɪˈvaɪs]	Stilmittel	
subject [ˈsʌbdʒekt]	Subjekt	*He* gave me a book. (cf. direct/indirect object)
subordinate clause [səˈbɔːdɪnət ˈklɔːz]	Nebensatz	relative clause, adverbial clause, *that*-clause, indirect question
substitutes (for modal auxiliaries) [ˈsʌbstɪtjuːts]	Ersatzformen (von modalen Hilfsverben)	I can swim. – I will *be able to* swim. You may go. – I *was allowed to* go.
suffix [ˈsʌfɪks]	Nachsilbe	teach*er*, move*ment*, nervous*ness*, etc.
superlative [suːˈpɜːlətɪv]	Superlativ	*best, fastest, most expensive*, etc.
tense [tens]	Zeitform	present tense, past tense, etc.
uncountable noun [ˌʌnˈkaʊntəbl ˈnaʊn]	nicht-zählbares Nomen	*water, coal, furniture, advice*, etc. (cf. countable noun)
verb [vɜːb]	Verb	*be, have, work, know*, etc.
verb of perception [pəˈsepʃn]	Verb der Wahrnehmung	*see, hear, feel, smell, taste, notice*
verbal expression [ˈvɜːbl ɪkˈspreʃn]	verbaler Ausdruck	*be fond of, be keen on, be likely to*, etc.
will-future [ˈwɪl ˌfjuːtʃə]	–	The weather *will change* tomorrow.
word formation [ˈwɜːd fɔːˈmeɪʃn]	Wortbildung	(e. g. *re-* + *write* → rewrite)
word order [ˈwɜːd ˌɔːdə]	Wortstellung	(e.g. subject – verb – object)
yes/no question	Entscheidungsfrage	*Do you like milk?* – Yes, I do./No, I don't.

8 British and American English

Differences in vocabulary

BE	AE	
lift	elevator	Aufzug
flat	apartment	Wohnung
caretaker	janitor	Hausmeister(in)
postman/ postwoman	mailman/ mailwoman	Briefträger(in)
shop	store	Geschäft, Laden
film	movie	Film
pavement	sidewalk	Bürgersteig
city centre	downtown	Stadtzentrum
underground	subway	U-Bahn
motorway	freeway	Autobahn
petrol	gas	Benzin
headmaster/ headmistress	principal	Schulleiter(in)
pupil	student	Schüler(in)
holidays	vacation	Ferien
trousers	pants	Hose
Mum	Mom	Mama
pocket money	allowance	Taschengeld
sweet	candy	Bonbon
biscuit	cookie	Keks
autumn	fall	Herbst
I suppose	I guess	ich glaube

Differences in spelling

BE	AE
col**our**, hon**our**, fav**our**	col**or**, hon**or**, fav**or**
cen**tre**, kilome**tre**	cen**ter**, kilome**ter**
travel**l**er, model**l**ing	trave**l**er, mode**l**ing
to fulfi**l**, ski**l**ful	to fulfi**ll**, ski**ll**ful
defe**nce**, lice**nce**	defe**nse**, lice**nse**
to analy**se**, to paraly**se**	to analy**ze**, to paraly**ze**
to practi**s**e	to practi**c**e
program**me**, che**que**, t**y**re	progra**m**, che**ck**, t**i**re
gr**e**y, Math**s**	gr**a**y, Ma**th**

Differences in pronunciation

ask, answer, can't	**BE:** [ɑː] **AE:** [æː]
new, duty, neutral	**BE:** [juː] **AE:** [uː]
either, neither	**BE:** [aɪ] **AE:** [iː]
sure, here, car	[r] in BE is only pronounced before a vowel; in AE it is always pronounced.
million, feeling	[l] in AE is pronounced as a 'dark' [l] even between vowels.
water, better	[t] in AE is pronounced 'weak' (i. e. rather like [d]) between vowels.
dog, John, boss	[ɒ] in AE has a more open pronunciation than in BE.

Index

The numbers here refer to the paragraphs. Example: 83.1 N 2 = § 83, section 1, note 2.
A number in bold print indicates the paragraph which deals with the particular word or structure in most detail.

Q